PROMISE KEEPERS®
MEN OF INTEGRITY

PROMISE BUILDERS™

— STUDY SERIES —

THE PROMISE KEEPER AT WORK

PUBLISHING
Colorado Springs, Colorado

CONTENTS

Foreword

The date was July 4, 1952. Later in the evening, fireworks would light up the skies across the United States. But before the festive celebrations, Florence Chadwick would attempt something never done by a woman. She would try to swim from Catalina Island to the mainland California coast.

The 21-mile swim through cold, shark-infested waters began on a dreary morning. As Chadwick waded into the Pacific saltwater, a thick fog prevented her from seeing clearly the boats in her own party. Millions watched on television as sharks circled so closely that they had to be driven away by rifle fire.

Imagine what Chadwick went through that day. She struggled against cold water, the fear of sharks, currents, and physical exhaustion. What do you think was her greatest enemy? Surprisingly, the fog proved to be her most formidable opponent.

Unfortunately, Chadwick couldn't complete her challenge. Less than one mile from the California coast, she was pulled from the water. Later, she said she hadn't been defeated by fatigue or even the numbing coldness of the water. Instead, the fog had beaten her. It obscured her goal, blinding her eyes, her heart, her reason. "I'm not excusing myself," she commented, "but if I could have seen the land, I might have made it."

I understand how she felt. I've never tried to swim the English Channel, as Chadwick did in both directions. Nor have I tried to swim from Catalina Island to the mainland California coast. But I have been numbed by the hassles and issues I've faced. And at times, the fog of this culture in which we live has obscured the goal of Christlikeness in my life. I'm sure you can identify as well.

Nowhere is the challenge of living for Jesus more evident than in the workplace. It's incredibly important for us to keep clearly in mind the goal He has set before us—that is, to display Him to those around us. Remember, we're not just doing our jobs; we're on assignment for Jesus Christ. As Tony Evans says, if you're a fireman, you're not just a fireman, but you're also God's representative in that department to show the people around you what God looks like when He's putting out a fire. If you're a doctor, you are God's representative in the medical field to demonstrate how He deals with people's pain and brokenness. If you're a financial planner, you're God's agent in that world to help people be good stewards of what He has entrusted to them.

The Bible studies in this book were

written by three guys who have helped many men in the workplace. These studies will aid you in keeping sight of the "land" of Christlikeness as you do your job day by day. They will take you on a journey of applying the seven promises of a Promise Keeper and showing your co-workers and others around you how Jesus would respond to the issues that come up in your working life. So for the next 48 weeks, with a group of similarly motivated men around you, let the Word of God help clear away the fog and keep your eyes clearly on Him.

Allow me to finish the story of Florence Chadwick. On a foggy September day in 1952, she waded back into the waters off Catalina Island. Two months before, she had failed in her attempt. Now she again faced a vision-obscuring fog. But this time, she saw the mainland coast in the recesses of her mind. And this time, she not only became the first woman to make the swim, but she also beat the *men's* record by two hours!

What had changed? Her attitude. She kept her mind focused on the land that lay beyond the fog, and she refused to give up.

Remember, "The one who is in you is greater than the one who is in the world" (1 John 4:4). Enjoy the Word of God, stay focused on Him, and you will never lose sight of the land.

Rodney L. Cooper
National Director for Education
Promise Keepers

ACKNOWLEDGMENTS

First and foremost, we give all the glory to our Lord, Jesus Christ.

This Promise Builders small-group study is the result of many talented individuals who pooled their skills and resources. We would like to recognize the following for their faithfulness:

- Bob Horner, Ron Ralston, and Dave Sunde, all from Marketplace Connections with Campus Crusade For Christ International, who wrote the studies.

- Larry Weeden with Focus on the Family, who edited the studies.

- Rob Johnson with Wilson-Johnson Creative for the cover design.

- Pete Richardson, Jim Gordon, and Mary Guenther from Promise Keepers.

The entire team is excited about the many ways God will work through you as you work through these studies.

INTRODUCTION

A sign of growth in the world of nature is change—change in the dimensions of a tree, fruit appearing on the vine, and flowers blooming in the garden. In a similar way, change for us means new levels of maturity, of understanding, and in the way we relate to our family and friends—truly being a Promise Keeper.

But what does it take for change to occur? In one word, time. Not just the ticking of the clock, but time that is given purposefully in this next year to study God's Word with brothers in Christ and become accountable to each other. Your life will be re-engineered week by week in the hour you invest in the group. The goal is not to make you a Bible scholar, but to help you learn to live with Jesus Christ as the center of your life, one day at a time.

This book contains 48 sessions of Bible studies for your small group—a year's supply. It is anticipated that your group will meet weekly except for unforeseen situations unique to your group.

Each weekly session is designed to take one hour. The questions for each session are answered interactively in the group. Open with fellowship around coffee and friendship, then allow **40 minutes** to interact with the biblical material. Use the final **10 minutes** for application and prayer. A small clock in each study will remind you to set aside those 10 minutes. A special *Prayer Journal* is provided to record the various requests week by week.

This may be your first time to participate in a weekly small group that meets for fellowship, Bible study, and prayer. Some men are hesitant to get involved simply because they're not sure where the group is going. In this case, we're seeking to take the next step from the stadium to the small group. We believe that when men gather in the name of Jesus Christ, Almighty God is pleased. And when they gather weekly to fellowship, pray, and apply God's Word, measurable change takes place. So call your friends. Pick a place to meet, and go for it!

"Be on your guard; stand firm in the faith; be men of courage; be strong. Do everything in love" (1 Corinthians 16:13).

Bob Horner
Ron Ralston
David Sunde

The Best Approach for Your Group

An Overview to Several Patterns of Men's Small-Group Bible Studies

Men who gather in a small group to fellowship, study the Bible, and pray together predictably follow one of several patterns. Often they aren't even aware of what their group has become, since they're accustomed to it. Of course, the leader of the group has tremendous influence in this area. The kind of group we have in mind for these sessions may call for some changes in the way you do things (if yours is an established group). But we hope you'll see the benefits of becoming a group that majors on interactive discussion and application of the timeless insights of God's Word.

"Adrift"

The Life Raft Group

This small group is made up of survivors—men who have survived a major battle in their lives. It may have been a recent battle or one from years ago. But the wounds and scars are reminders of what each has suffered. What began as an emergency situation has turned into a weekly meeting. So each man is just happy to be among his friends. Life raft groups really have no leader—each man has his own story to tell around some biblical idea or paragraph. Of concern to the men is that they're adrift. And though high on encouragement, they're low on long-term biblical resources.

"Feeling Good"
THE YACHT GROUP

If you long to feel good among friends, climb aboard this craft! The skipper will welcome you with a hot cup of coffee or whatever else you'd like. Each man needs a Bible, of course—and the study will begin as soon as they push off. But meanwhile, they'll just enjoy the Lord and each other. For some reason, the seagoing stories of fellow mariners always take more time than the skipper planned for, so time in the Word will resume next week. Your need to move beyond the fellowship—to get into the Word—may urge you on to see what other boats are in the harbor.

"Battle Weary"
THE DESTROYER GROUP

This pattern is named after the naval vessel of the same class. It's a warship, armed and ready for battle against the forces of evil in society and our lives. Disciplined Bible study is the order of the day. Truth from Scripture is fired from the leader like missiles from the deck launchers. Some of the sailors look as if they have taken direct hits from the Word, but the leader has properly warned them that such are the costs of discipleship. No one questions the reality of spiritual warfare, though the battle-weary men sense the need for some spiritual support from the Lord.

"Deep and Long: Where Are We?"	"Refreshed, Refueled, Refocused"
### THE SUBMARINE GROUP	### THE CARRIER GROUP

"Deep and Long: Where Are We?"
THE SUBMARINE GROUP

To the captain of the sub, there are just two kinds of boats: subs and targets. Aboard this kind of small group, Bible study gives the experience of going down deep, staying down long, and, after a while, wondering where you really are. A life of disciplined study is essential if you're to last with this group. And you may not be sure the captain likes you, but you know you're investing time in a highly strategic activity, below the surface of life. If it's fellowship balanced with interactive Bible study and prayer you're looking for, however, you'd better not go down the ladder into the sub group.

"Refreshed, Refueled, Refocused"
THE CARRIER GROUP

An aircraft carrier is a warship equipped with a large open deck for the taking off and landing of warplanes. As well, it's equipped to carry, service, and arm its planes. A small-group Bible study in this pattern is on a mission, under way to be in strategic position for the men on board. Each time the men come, in the midst of the work week, they know they will be refreshed, refueled, and refocused for life's battles and open seas. They leave ready to fulfill the biblical plan they studied, alert to serve their Captain well. This kind of small group is what we have in mind for the sessions ahead. Of course there is value in the other kinds of group patterns, but we believe that the aircraft carrier model best serves our goal of becoming Promise Builders in the year before us.

LEADER'S GUIDELINES

FOR BUILDING A SUCCESSFUL PROMISE
BUILDERS MEN'S GROUP

Leaders of small-group Bible studies have traditionally been people of superior biblical knowledge and (hopefully) great spiritual maturity. But in Promise Builders small groups, we're changing some of the rules. Our leaders are meant to be facilitators, not biblical experts. The purpose of the Promise Builder group leader is to encourage discussion and interaction. Thus, he is more a coach than a commentator. In other words, the group is meant to be leader-light.

There are, however, a few other responsibilities for the leader:

• Start and end each session on time. This shows respect for the men and their duties.

• Pray for group members by name before each meeting.

• Value each man's comments and insights.

• Secure a meeting place, preferably in the marketplace rather than a home or church—some place like the back of a restaurant, a cafeteria, a conference room, a community center, or someone's office.

• Work closely with the men who are facilitating the group in other ways, such as the timekeepers, the prayer leader, and the calendar coordinator.

Following these simple guidelines, plus the carrier-group mind-set described earlier and the session game plan given in the Introduction, will help you and the other men in your group to see life-changing results as you go through the studies in this book.

The Promise Keeper at Work

A godly man at work faces a great challenge. He's a representative of Jesus Christ in a place where the name of the Lord may be only a curse word. Or there may be the attitude that one's personal faith is just that—personal, and not to be discussed in the workplace. What is God's man to do?

Your own workplace, on the other hand, may be very supportive of what you believe. But your question may be, Where do I start in representing the One who is becoming the center of my life? How can I have an *impact* in the lives of those around me on the job?

We have some answers! *The Promise Keeper at Work* is more than a year's worth of interactive Bible studies for small groups. *It provides a strategy for making an impact in your workplace.* As you move progressively through the weeks of study, an equipping process is going on. The best way we know to picture where these studies will lead is with a set of concentric circles.

The core circle: *Walk.* The goal in this section of studies is to equip you in the basics of a daily relationship with Jesus Christ. We're calling it your *walk with the Lord.* A meaningful and growing walk will be centered in God's Word. That's the primary way He speaks to us. It then follows that if we're to have a quality walk with Him, we need to communicate with Him daily. So prayer is the next focus of study. Finally, the power to achieve God's will, as it's discovered in the Word and in prayer, comes from the Holy Spirit. It's essential that we're rightly related to His powerful presence within us. The beginning of our impact for Christ is in our daily *walk* with Him.

The second circle: *Work.* Building a good reputation in the workplace has everything to do with the quality of our job performance. In this section of Bible studies, the goal is to equip you in both your perspective on, and your attitude toward, work.

The third circle: *Relationships.* The Good News of Jesus Christ travels on the network of relationships in the workplace. We need to follow biblical guidelines for winning friends and influencing people on the job. Naturally, we'll have to overcome some barriers to make good relationships a part of our workplace. But whatever it takes to build a bridge to those with whom you work, you'll be doing what Jesus would do if He were in your shoes.

The fourth circle: *Ministry.* People need the Lord. The marketplace is one of the most neglected areas of outreach. How will our fellow workers ever hear of new life in Jesus? It's our great opportunity to introduce them to Him. But that's just the beginning!

We can also help new Christians grow in the Lord and become a part of the church.

It's our prayer that as you go

through these studies with your small group, you'll be both equipped and motivated to take up the challenge of being God's man and making a difference for Him every day in your place of work.

MISSION STATEMENT

Promise Keepers is a Christ-centered ministry dedicated to uniting men through vital relationships to become godly influences in their world.

THE SEVEN PROMISES

OF A PROMISE KEEPER

1 **A man and his God.**
A Promise Keeper is committed to honor Jesus Christ through worship, prayer, and obedience to God's Word in the power of the Holy Spirit.

2 **A man and his friends.**
A Promise Keeper is committed to pursue vital relationships with a few other men, understanding that he needs brothers to help him keep his promises.

3 **A man and his integrity.**
A Promise Keeper is committed to practice spiritual, moral, ethical, and sexual purity.

4 **A man and his family.**
A Promise Keeper is committed to build strong marriages and families through love, protection, and biblical values.

5 **A man and his church.**
A Promise Keeper is committed to support the mission of his church by honoring and praying for his pastors and by actively giving his time and resources.

6 **A man and his brothers.**
A Promise Keeper is committed to reach beyond any racial and denominational barriers to demonstrate the power of biblical unity.

7 **A man and his world.**
A Promise Keeper is committed to influence his world, being obedient to the Great Commandment (see Mark 12:30-31) and the Great Commission (see Matthew 28:19-20).

PLUMB LINE FOR A CROOKED CULTURE

FIRST IN THE SERIES ON THE WORD

WARM-UP: LARRY'S CONSTRUCTION BUSINESS HAS BEEN REVOLUTIONIZED IN RECENT YEARS BY THE INTRODUCTION OF THE LASER. ITS ACCURACY IS UNEQUALED—AT ANY DISTANCE. LARRY SAYS HIS BRICKLAYERS NOW HAVE PERFECTLY STRAIGHT LINES TO FOLLOW. OFFICE CEILINGS ARE HUNG IN RECORD TIME, YET THEY ARE TRULY LEVEL. OTHER TOOLS ARE CONSIDERED OUTDATED AND CLUMSY WHEN COMPARED TO THE SPEED AND SIMPLICITY OF THIS INDUSTRIAL LASER. WHAT OTHER MEASURING DEVICES ARE AVAILABLE TO HELP INSURE ACCURACY AND MEET STANDARDS?

BACKGROUND

Prison is the last place from which to expect a letter of encouragement, but that's where Paul's second letter to Timothy originated. Timothy was encouraged not to waver in using Scripture to identify and describe both the doctrinal error and the moral evil so pervasive in his culture. Each of us can use this kind of encouragement for our days within a culture also dominated by doctrinal error and moral evil.

WALK ⇨

READ

2 TIMOTHY 3:1-17

QUESTIONS FOR INTERACTION:

1 In light of what Paul said about the first-century culture in which he and Timothy lived, what would have been so challenging about following biblical standards?

2 The most powerful form of teaching about standards is the life of someone who models what's right. In what way was Paul a role model for Timothy?

PROMISE KEEPERS®
MEN OF INTEGRITY

3 Beyond the benefit of a good role model, how did the Scriptures enable Timothy to relate to his culture?

4 What are four purposes for the Word of God in our lives? (verse 16)

5 Describe the person who ignores the Word of God in his life.

WRAP-UP: EACH MAN IDENTIFY AND DESCRIBE A PERSON WHO EMBRACES THE WORD OF GOD AS A MEASURING STANDARD IN HIS OR HER LIFE.

 LET'S PRAY: (SEE PRAYER JOURNAL)

. . . .

MY RESPONSE AS A PROMISE KEEPER

What will it take to get and keep me in the Word of God regularly?

In light of the importance of His Word to me, I will spend _____ minutes each day this week in the Word.

MIRROR, MIRROR ON THE WALL

SECOND IN THE SERIES ON THE WORD

. . . .

WARM-UP: WHILE A TALKING, ALL-KNOWING MIRROR EXISTS ONLY IN THE IMAGINATION OF A FANTASY MOVIE, A MIRROR ACTUALLY DOES TELL US A GREAT DEAL. HAS MY HAIR GOTTEN TOO LONG? WHERE ON MY HEAD WOULD I LIKE SOME HAIR? WHAT'S THAT ON MY TIE? AND IF I CHOOSE TO IGNORE WHAT MY MIRROR IS TELLING ME, THAT DOESN'T MEAN THE PROBLEM HAS BEEN CORRECTED. WHY DO WE TEND TO IGNORE SOME THINGS WE SEE IN OUR MIRRORS?

BACKGROUND

The church over which James presided in A.D. 55 had a problem with hearing the Word of God but not doing it. Sounds a lot like the Christianity of our day, doesn't it? Historically, moving from knowledge to action has always been a challenge . . . and a serious problem.

READ

JAMES 1:19-25

QUESTIONS FOR INTERACTION:

1 It's common to hear the Word and yet be unresponsive to it. How can we explain this?

2 Our culture gives free expression to anger, filthiness, and wickedness. What does James call us to do in light of that?

(WALK) ⇨

3 Why is an attitude of humility essential in receiving the Word's message in light of our culture?

4 Describe a person you know (no names, please) who has not been responsive to the mirror of God's Word.

5 Describe a person you know who *has* been responsive to the mirror of God's Word.

WRAP-UP. DISCUSS TOGETHER HOW YOU WOULD HELP SOMEONE MOVE FROM HEARING TO DOING THE WORD OF GOD.

 LET'S PRAY: (SEE PRAYER JOURNAL)

● ●

MY RESPONSE AS A PROMISE KEEPER

What steps can I take this week to be more of a doer of the Word and not just a hearer? _____

_____

FOLLOW THE YELLOW BRICK ROAD

THIRD IN THE SERIES ON THE WORD

WARM-UP: CROSS-COUNTRY TRAVEL ON A FAMILY VACATION CAN DRIVE THE KIDS NUTS WITH IMPATIENCE. THEY CONTINUALLY ASK, "ARE WE THERE YET?" OR "DADDY, HOW MANY MORE TOWNS?" UNLESS CHILDREN GRASP THE CONCEPT OF A ROAD MAP, THEY HAVE NO PERSPECTIVE ON HOW LONG IT TAKES— OR BY WHAT ROUTE—TO GET FROM POINT A TO POINT B. WHAT ARE YOU, THE DRIVER, DOING WITH A MAP THAT YOUR CHILDREN AREN'T?

BACKGROUND

Psalm 119 is the longest of all the psalms. Although we're not sure who wrote it, the writer was passionately devoted to the Word of God as the word of life. All but three verses mention the Bible in some way: ordinances, promises, statutes, commandments, and the Law. The section for our study today addresses meditating on Scripture, which produces the highest wisdom possible, becoming tuned to the mind of God.

READ

PSALM 119:97-112

QUESTIONS FOR INTERACTION:

1 What part of your newspaper would you say is your "morning meditation"? Why? Why would the psalmist say he loved the Word of God so much as to meditate on it?

2 How does the Word enlighten the person seeking to walk with God?

(WALK) ⇨

3 Why is a solid commitment to obey the Word—even when hard to swallow—a part of the guidance process?

4 The pathway of the Lord's will is not necessarily smooth. What did the psalmist do with the Word to sustain him in turbulent times?

5 What happens to us when we make a lifelong commitment to the timeless insights of Scripture?

WRAP-UP: BASED ON TODAY'S DISCUSSION, HOW WOULD YOU USE THE BIBLE AS A "MAP" TO HELP A FRIEND WHO IS SEEKING TO KNOW THE LORD'S WILL REGARDING A JOB CHANGE?

LET'S PRAY: (SEE PRAYER JOURNAL)

MY RESPONSE AS A PROMISE KEEPER

What are some of the benefits of packing a Bible in my carry-on when traveling? _____

_____

What might regular Bible reading and discussion do for my personal life, business life, and family life? _____

_____

PURE DELIGHT

FOURTH IN THE SERIES ON THE WORD

● ●

WARM-UP: AS A HIGH-SCHOOL BASKETBALL COACH AND FORMER PROFESSIONAL PLAYER, DAVE WAS GETTING MORE AND MORE FRUSTRATED WITH HIS MOST-GIFTED ATHLETE. CURTIS HAD INCREDIBLE NATURAL ABILITY BUT FELT HE HAD NOTHING MORE TO LEARN. HIS TEAMMATES, ON THE OTHER HAND, SOAKED UP EVERY WORD DAVE OFFERED, BECAUSE THEY WANTED TO EMULATE THEIR COACH AND BECOME SUCCESSFUL BASKETBALL PLAYERS. HOW MIGHT WE HELP COACH DAVE?

BACKGROUND

A teachable spirit is of great value in the sight of God and man. A person who has such a spirit desires to live pleasing to God and in harmonious relationship with his or her associates. How do we develop a teachable spirit? The section of Scripture in focus today tells us what to value in becoming such a person.

READ

PSALM 119:9-16

QUESTIONS FOR INTERACTION:

1 Why do you think the psalmist specified young men as the ones who need the Word of God to keep their way pure?

2 Why must we not be halfhearted when we seek the Lord to keep our way pure?

WALK ⇒

PROMISE KEEPERS®
MEN OF INTEGRITY

3 How does treasuring Scripture help deter the power of sin in our lives?

4 Agree/disagree: If I were to win an $8,000,000 lottery, I would need the Lord less. How would the psalmist answer this?

5 What commitments of time and energy does the psalmist model that will bring the Word into our daily lives?

WRAP-UP:
BRAINSTORM IDEAS ON HOW THIS PROMISE BUILDER GROUP CAN HELP US TO REACH OUR POTENTIAL IN GOD'S EYES.

LET'S PRAY: (SEE PRAYER JOURNAL)

MY RESPONSE AS A PROMISE KEEPER

When do I know I have not treasured the Word of God in my heart?

_____

What steps do I need to take to launch the treasuring of Scripture?

_____

THE MIDNIGHT VISITOR

FIRST IN THE SERIES ON PRAYER

WARM-UP: BILL PRAYED FOR 45 YEARS FOR HIS SON, NICK, TO BECOME A CHRISTIAN. SADLY, BILL DIED WITHOUT SEEING HIS PRAYERS ANSWERED. HOWEVER, ONE YEAR AFTER HIS FATHER'S DEATH, NICK DID OPEN HIS LIFE TO JESUS CHRIST. TO THIS DAY, WHEN NICK TELLS HIS STORY, HE SAYS HE CAME TO KNOW THE LORD BECAUSE HIS FATHER PRAYED FOR HIM EVERY DAY OF HIS LIFE. HE REMEMBERS HIS FATHER AS A MAN WHO PRAYED FAITHFULLY AND PERSISTENTLY. WHAT DISCOURAGES US FROM BEING PERSISTENT IN OUR PRAYERS?

BACKGROUND

Today's paragraph for study is almost halfway into Luke's Gospel. Why did the disciples take so long to ask Jesus about prayer? He graciously gave them a simple model to follow, however. Because of their religious culture, His disciples would have prayed in a more formal way, likely referring to God in terms that tended to put Him at a distance. However, Jesus taught them to now think of God as their Father in heaven who is responsive to their needs.

READ

LUKE 11:1-13

QUESTIONS FOR INTERACTION:

1 What do you think motivated Jesus' disciples to ask Him for instruction regarding prayer?

2 What is so masterful about the answer Jesus gave? What's significant about addressing God as Father?

(WALK) ⇨

PROMISE KEEPERS®
MEN OF INTEGRITY

3 What do you think Jesus expected the disciples to do with this prayer? What do you think Jesus *didn't* expect the disciples to do with it?

4 Why do you think Jesus told the story of the midnight visitor?

5 Why is persistence in prayer difficult?

WRAP-UP:
SELECT ONE OR TWO ISSUES/NEEDS IN THE GROUP, AND PRAY TOGETHER ABOUT THEM.

LET'S PRAY: (SEE PRAYER JOURNAL)

MY RESPONSE AS A PROMISE KEEPER

What or who motivates me to pray? Why? _____

_____

How can I overcome my natural reluctance to persevere in prayer? _____

_____

So, You're Too Busy to Pray!

SECOND IN THE SERIES ON PRAYER

WARM-UP: WHAT IS YOUR FIRST PRIORITY OF THE DAY? STEWART IS A METICULOUS MAN WHO TAKES CARE OF HIMSELF, HIS BUSINESS, AND HIS HOME. EACH DAY IS A RACE TO SEE IF HE CAN "CHECK OFF" HIS DAILY PRIORITIES. A GOOD DAY FOR STEWART IS WHEN HE GOES TO BED FEELING A SENSE OF ACCOMPLISHMENT. HOWEVER, HE RARELY FINDS TIME TO PRAY. FOR MANY OF US, THE FIRST APPOINTMENT WE MISS AS WE HEAD INTO A BUSY DAY IS A QUIET TIME WITH THE LORD. WHY IS IT USUALLY THE FIRST TO GO?

BACKGROUND

The Gospel of Mark is often described as the action account of the life of Jesus. In today's section for study, we'll see just how full His life could get as He went about His work. Surely His schedule could match that of anyone in our day in terms of pressure and stress. Yet He wasn't too busy to pray. How did Jesus find the time? This session will help us refocus our perspective so we can pray amid pressured times.

(WALK) ⇨

READ

MARK 1:16-39

QUESTIONS FOR INTERACTION:

1 What activities filled the busy life of Jesus as told by Mark in his first chapter, and what might have contributed to exhaustion?

2 Why do you think it was so important to Jesus to not miss quality time with His Father?

PROMISE KEEPERS®
MEN OF INTEGRITY

26

3 In light of Jesus' example, why is "I'm just too busy" not a good enough excuse for our lack of prayer?

4 What were the essential components of the quiet time to Jesus, as described in verse 35?

WRAP-UP. CONTRAST THE WAY PETER AND JESUS BEGAN A NEW DAY, AS NOTED BY MARK IN 1:36-37.

SOME OF US JUST AREN'T "MORNING PEOPLE." HOW ARE WE TO DUPLICATE OUR LORD'S PATTERN?

 LET'S PRAY: (SEE PRAYER JOURNAL)

● ●

MY RESPONSE AS A PROMISE KEEPER

Why do I find it difficult to make time to pray? _____

_____

I will make prayer a priority in my daily schedule this next week, beginning with Monday, Wednesday, and Friday mornings before work.

LIP-SERVICE PRAYERS: KISS THEM GOOD-BYE!

THIRD IN THE SERIES ON PRAYER

WARM-UP: AL ALWAYS MAKES IT A POINT TO PRAY WITH HIS FAMILY IN PUBLIC, WHETHER IT BE AT MEALS, CHURCH, OR SOCIAL FUNCTIONS. BUT HE DOES THIS TO SHOW OTHER PEOPLE WHAT A GOOD CHRISTIAN HE IS. WHAT IS THE DANGER OF PRAYING AUDIBLY IN PUBLIC?

BACKGROUND

The religious culture of Jesus' day was a reflection of the synagogue leaders. Those men made public show of their giving to the needy and the saying of prayers. They proudly prayed with long, repetitive phrases as a measure of their supposed righteousness. Likely many Jewish worshipers had adopted their hypocritical patterns. But Jesus offered His followers a new and meaningful way to pray to the Father in heaven.

(WALK) ⇨

READ

MATTHEW 6:5-8

QUESTIONS FOR INTERACTION:

1 We need good models for developing our prayer life. What was seriously lacking in the prayer patterns of Jesus' day?

2 Why do you think Jesus began His teaching on prayer with negative models?

PROMISE KEEPERS® MEN OF INTEGRITY

3 Describe the manner of prayer Jesus advocated. Why would the Father prefer this approach?

4 What did Jesus find objectionable with prayers of repetition? What's the difference between repetition and perseverance?

WRAP-UP: IF YOU COULD COUNSEL AL AFTER TODAY'S SESSION, WHAT WOULD YOU TELL HIM?

 LET'S PRAY: (SEE PRAYER JOURNAL)

● ●

MY RESPONSE AS A PROMISE KEEPER

What should change in my prayers as a result of today's study? _____

_____

I will give five minutes to private prayer each day this week.

WHY PRAY WHEN YOU CAN WORRY?

FOURTH IN THE SERIES ON PRAYER

• •

WARM-UP: RALPH RUNS A LARGE TRUCKING FIRM THAT DELIVERS HIGHLY PERISHABLE PRODUCE ACROSS A THREE-STATE REGION. HIS DRIVERS ARE ALL UNION MEN. RALPH HAS JUST LEARNED THAT THEIR UNION IS PLANNING AN IMMEDIATE NATIONAL STRIKE. HE WONDERS HOW HE'LL KEEP HIS PRODUCE FROM ROTTING ON THE LOADING DOCKS. TALK TOGETHER ABOUT HIS OPTIONS . . . AND HIS ANXIETY.

BACKGROUND

The number-one by-product of our culture is anxiety. Stress disorders are experienced in nearly every household. The apostle Paul, in his letter to the Philippian church, was keenly aware that circumstances and people do an outside job on us, but anxiety is the inside villain. In today's study, he gives us some needed encouragement and a plan to cope.

READ

PHILIPPIANS 4:6-9

QUESTIONS FOR INTERACTION:

1 What is anxiety? Why is it so commonplace? What does it do to us?

2 Why might some readers of this letter think Paul's words were not in touch with reality: "Do not be anxious about anything"?

PROMISE KEEPERS®
MEN OF INTEGRITY

3 What is Paul's plan for letting go of much of life's anxiety?

4 Why is thanksgiving included in the process of releasing anxiety?

5 What replaces anxiety in the life of the person who prays this way? How would you describe it?

6 Why is it important for our hearts and minds to be guarded?

WRAP-UP. EACH MAN DESCRIBE A PRESSURE HE IS FACING AND WHAT IT MIGHT BE DOING TO HIS HEART OR MIND RIGHT NOW.

LET'S PRAY: (SEE PRAYER JOURNAL)

MY RESPONSE AS A PROMISE KEEPER

What are some reasons I may not have followed the Lord's plan to release anxiety? _____

_____

What new steps will I take today when anxiety strikes? _____

_____

"I JUST DON'T GET IT!"

FIRST IN THE SERIES ON POWER

WARM-UP: KEVIN'S WIFE ATTENDS A WEEKLY WOMEN'S BIBLE STUDY. WHENEVER SHE TELLS HIM HOW MUCH SHE ENJOYS IT, KEVIN THINKS, "I JUST DON'T GET IT. HOW CAN ANYONE GET ANYTHING OUT OF THE BIBLE?"

BACKGROUND

The city of Corinth was not only well known for its immorality and nightlife, but it had also drunk deeply of the intellectual side of Greek culture. Corinthians prized the insights of wisdom. Because the apostle Paul refused to go along with them, he was judged as simplistic. His response to such an accusation is discovered in today's section for study. He had resources of wisdom they would never know naturally.

READ

1 CORINTHIANS 2:6-16

QUESTIONS FOR INTERACTION:

1 How is it that so often a man does not understand God and His Word?

2 What new dimensions can open up to us because God has given us His Spirit?

WALK ⇨

PROMISE
K E E P E R S ®
MEN OF INTEGRITY

3 A Christian friend says, "And if I am not in the habit of learning from God's Spirit, so what?" How would you respond?

4 What subjects are popular among worldly men in the marketplace? How are conversations between spiritual men likely to be different?

WRAP-UP. DISCUSS TOGETHER HOW OUR BIBLE STUDY AND CHRISTIAN LIFE WILL CHANGE AS WE ALLOW GOD'S SPIRIT TO INSTRUCT US.

 LET'S PRAY: (SEE PRAYER JOURNAL)

MY RESPONSE AS A PROMISE KEEPER

My Bible study can never be the same after today. From now on, I must depend upon the Holy Spirit to teach me and give me understanding.

NEEDLE ON "FULL"

SECOND IN THE SERIES ON POWER

WARM-UP: WHATEVER FILLS US, CONTROLS US. IF WE'RE FILLED WITH ANGER, WE'RE CONTROLLED BY IT. IF WE'RE FILLED WITH JOY, OUR EMOTIONS ANNOUNCE THEIR DELIGHT. IF OUR SCHEDULES FILL OUR LIVES, WE'RE CONTROLLED BY THEM. DISCUSS TOGETHER WHAT THINGS FILL OUR LIVES PRESENTLY. WHAT EFFECT DOES THIS HAVE ON US AND ON THOSE AROUND US?

BACKGROUND

What fills our lives? Many answers come to mind, depending on our perspective. It could be our work schedule, our children's activities, the anticipation of a job change, or even an approaching vacation. However we respond, another answer is given in today's section for study and interaction. It is the filling of the Holy Spirit. Many followers of Christ are unclear what this means. However, when God's Spirit is filling our lives, we can never be the same as we were before!

READ

EPHESIANS 5:15-21

QUESTIONS FOR INTERACTION:

1 What does it mean to walk wisely?

2 Why has God designed our lives to be filled with His presence?

WALK ⇨

3 Why do you think the apostle Paul contrasted being controlled by the Holy Spirit with being controlled by wine?

4 What does the apostle tell us will be the clear evidence that one is filled with the Holy Spirit? (see verses 19-21)

WRAP-UP: TOGETHER COME UP WITH A PRAYER THAT YOU CAN USE REGULARLY TO INVITE THE HOLY SPIRIT TO FILL, OR CONTROL, YOUR THOUGHTS, WORDS, AND ACTIONS.

 LET'S PRAY: (SEE PRAYER JOURNAL)

MY RESPONSE AS A PROMISE KEEPER

By faith in God's command, each day I will ask His Holy Spirit to fill me, resulting in new responses in my relationships at work.

TWO-PART HARMONY

• •

WARM-UP.

AFTER DINNER, JERRY IS RELAXING IN THE FAMILY ROOM FOR A FEW MIN-
UTES, READING THE SPORTS PAGE. HE CAN'T HELP HEARING HIS TWO SONS,
WHOSE BICKERING IS ESCALATING. WHAT MUST JERRY BE FEELING AT THIS
MOMENT?

BACKGROUND

It's easy to think first-century believers lived in harmony since they were so close to the time of Jesus. But in today's study, we'll look at a group of Christians in Ephesus who struggled in getting along and, in doing so, dishonored the Lord and saddened His Spirit. If He is honored in our lives, however, He will empower us to attain new levels of fellowship.

READ

EPHESIANS
4:25—5:2

QUESTIONS FOR INTERACTION:

1 What must have been going on among the believers in Ephesus?

2 What was the impact of this kind of behavior on each other—and on the Holy Spirit?

WALK ⇨

3 List and discuss ways the apostle Paul advised those struggling believers to build harmony.

4 What might be grieving the Holy Spirit among the believers you know?

5 How can we apply the apostle's instructions in our workplaces?

WRAP-UP. SILENTLY AND INDIVIDUALLY PRAY: "LORD, IS ANYTHING IN MY LIFE GRIEVING YOU?" (IF THERE IS SOMETHING, THE HOLY SPIRIT WILL BRING IT TO MIND QUICKLY.) SOMEONE CLOSE AFTER FIVE MINUTES.

LET'S PRAY: (SEE PRAYER JOURNAL)

● ●

MY RESPONSE AS A PROMISE KEEPER

How am I to live in harmony with others and with the Holy Spirit?

_____

_____

WALKATHON

FOURTH IN THE SERIES ON POWER

● ●

WARM-UP: MATT SOUNDS LIKE EVERYONE ELSE ON HIS CONSTRUCTION CREW. HIS LANGUAGE IS JUST AS COARSE AND CRUDE. HOWEVER, MATT IS A CHRISTIAN AND IS TROUBLED BY HIS LANGUAGE ON THE JOB. WHEN IT BEGAN TO LEAK INTO HIS HOME LIFE, HE KNEW HE MUST DO SOMETHING ABOUT IT. ONE EARLY MORNING, HE DISCOVERED SOMETHING IN HIS NEW TESTAMENT THAT GAVE HIM HOPE THAT HE COULD CHANGE. OUR PASSAGE TODAY WAS LIKELY THE FOCUS OF MATT'S STUDY.

BACKGROUND

We would like to think we're independent, unaffected by whatever forces arise against us. However, in the real world, we face two opposite and powerful forces every day; both seek to control us. They are the flesh (our natural bent) and the Spirit (the Holy Spirit of God). Even though we, as believers, are indwelled by God's Holy Spirit, we face the choice of how we will walk—in the power of the flesh or in the power of the Spirit. This could be a life-changing day as we choose to walk in the power of God's great gift: His Holy Spirit.

 WALK ⇨

READ

GALATIANS 5:16-26

QUESTIONS FOR INTERACTION:

1 Describe a person who is walking by the flesh. (No names, please.)

Describe a person who is walking by the Spirit.

2 One translation defines "walk in the Spirit" as "Live freely, animated and motivated by God's Spirit." In choosing to live by the Spirit, what is always in tension?

PROMISE
KEEPERS®
MEN OF INTEGRITY

3 Agree or disagree with this statement, and explain why: "Walk by the Spirit and you will not carry out the desires of the flesh."

4 How do we explain the fact that so many Christians apparently do not walk by the Spirit?

5 The how-to of walking by the Spirit is choosing to live daily in dependence on Him and His power. Why did the apostle refer to the results of walking by the Spirit as "fruit"?

WRAP-UP: GO AROUND THE GROUP, AND EACH MAN STATE WHICH PART OF THE SPIRIT'S FRUIT HE WOULD MOST LIKE GOD TO MATURE IN HIS WORK LIFE. WHEN YOU PRAY TOGETHER, EACH PRAY SPECIFICALLY FOR THE REQUEST OF THE MAN ON HIS RIGHT.

LET'S PRAY: (SEE PRAYER JOURNAL)

MY RESPONSE AS A PROMISE KEEPER

I will memorize Galatians 5:22-23 and meditate on the fruit of the Spirit this week.

I will seek closer association with those I know who walk in the Spirit.

TGIM: Thank God It's Monday!

First in the series on the Biblical Basis for Work

WARM-UP: THE GRADUATING CLASS WAITED EAGERLY TO HEAR THE COMMENCEMENT ADDRESS FROM MALCOLM FORBES, THE BILLIONAIRE PUBLISHER. THEY ALL EXPECTED GREAT WISDOM ON HOW TO BECOME WEALTHY. INSTEAD, HOW- EVER, THEY WERE STUNNED WHEN FORBES SIMPLY SAID, "AS YOU STEP INTO THE MARKETPLACE, WORK AT SOMETHING YOU ENJOY. IF YOU ENJOY WHAT YOU DO, SUCCESS WILL FOLLOW." TAKE A MINUTE TO DESCRIBE TO THE GROUP THE MOST ENJOYABLE JOB YOU EVER HAD.

BACKGROUND

Most workers say on Friday morning, "TGIF!" Another work week is about to become history. Whether you love your job or are just tolerating it, there's a universal intuition that life has got to be more than work. Many Christians in the work- place think this way, too. Why not? But today's ses- sion will help us rethink work. As amazing as it sounds, one outcome of this study could be that, come Monday next week, you'll say, "TGIM."

READ

GENESIS 1:26— 2:3,15

QUESTIONS FOR INTERACTION:

1 What are some reasons we might say, "Thank God it's Friday"?

2 Why do you think God's plan for our lives includes work?

3 How has the culture (even our Christian culture) affected our view of work?

4 When God viewed His work, He saw it as "very good." Viewing your work, what would it take for you to say the same thing?

5 What reasons are there in today's Bible passage for saying that work was not given as a curse on mankind?

WRAP-UP: AS A RESULT OF TODAY'S STUDY, WHAT ARE SOME REASONS WE MIGHT NOW SAY, "THANK GOD IT'S MONDAY"?

LET'S PRAY: (SEE PRAYER JOURNAL)
BEGIN PRAYING BY EACH MAN THANKING GOD FOR HIS OWN WORK.

• •

MY RESPONSE AS A PROMISE KEEPER

I will begin each day this week by thanking God for my work.

I will begin my workday on Monday with, "TGIM!"

TAKE THIS JOB AND SHOVEL IT!

SECOND IN THE SERIES ON THE
BIBLICAL BASIS FOR WORK

• •

WARM-UP: DAN ISSEL, AS THE NEW COACH OF THE DENVER NUGGETS, HELPED TURN THE FRANCHISE AROUND. BUT NOT EVEN THE SUCCESS OF THE TEAM—OR HIS SIX-FIGURE SALARY—COULD KEEP HIM THERE TO COMPLETE HIS CONTRACT. IN MID-SEASON, HE SHOCKED THE PLAYERS AND FANS BY ANNOUNCING, "FOR PERSONAL REASONS, I QUIT." WHAT MIGHT HAVE BEEN SOME REASONS THIS SUCCESSFUL COACH WOULD LEAVE SUCH A LUCRATIVE AND HIGH-PROFILE JOB?

BACKGROUND

The Bible says God never considered work to be a curse on mankind. Nonetheless, there's a vague feeling among both Christians and those still searching for God that work is a curse. Today's section for study takes a long-needed closer look at the curse that did fall on the human race. If it wasn't work, what was it? That's the discovery before us.

READ

GENESIS 2:15-17; 3:1-24

QUESTIONS FOR INTERACTION:

1 What might make a skilled worker begin to say, "I don't like to go to work anymore"?

2 In Genesis 2:15-17, the will of the Creator was spelled out for Adam and Eve. What was it? Why might some think this was too confining?

3 How could this couple be so deceived by a talking snake?

4 Several curses fell on those in the garden. In particular, what was the curse on Adam?

5 Why is it commonly thought that work was the curse of the sin of Adam and Eve?

WRAP-UP: WHAT DIFFERENCES DO YOU SEE BETWEEN ADAM'S AND EVE'S WORK IN GENESIS 2 AND GENESIS 3?

LET'S PRAY: (SEE PRAYER JOURNAL)

MY RESPONSE AS A PROMISE KEEPER

How can I bring God's perspective on work into my workplace this week?

_____

The "thorns and thistles" that make work hard for me are: _____

_____

I will begin replacing them with these appropriate attitudes and responses:

_____

43

"I Owe, I Owe, So Off to Work I Go!"

THIRD IN THE SERIES ON THE BIBLICAL BASIS FOR WORK

WARM-UP: YEARS AGO, A LARGE CATHEDRAL WAS BEING BUILT IN EUROPE. AS IT NEARED COMPLETION, THREE OF THE BRICKLAYERS WERE ASKED WHY THEY WERE WILLING TO RISK THEIR LIVES LAYING BRICKS AT SUCH HEIGHTS. THE FIRST SAID, "BECAUSE I NEED TO EARN WAGES TO FEED MY FAMILY." THE SECOND SAID, "BECAUSE I AM THE BEST BRICKLAYER IN TOWN, SO I MUST BE HERE." AND THE THIRD SAID, "BECAUSE I AM HELPING TO BUILD A GREAT HOUSE OF WORSHIP TO OUR GOD."

IF SOMEONE WERE TO ASK WHY YOU GO TO WORK, WHAT WOULD YOU SAY? EACH MAN RESPOND.

BACKGROUND

Unfortunately for many people, their work means nothing more than "I owe, I owe . . ." We would like to escape the pressure of having to work, but few have any alternative. Even though work is a major part of our daily lives, all of us have asked, at some time or another, "What's the meaning of it all?" Does work have some redeeming value other than providing a paycheck? The answer awaits us as we consider the wise insights of an ancient king.

READ

ECCLESIASTES 2:1-26

QUESTIONS FOR INTERACTION:

1 How far did Solomon go to discover the meaning of life and work? Why do you think he pursued this with such passion?

2 What was so frustrating to the king concerning work? Why?

3 Why do you think King Solomon described one's work life in terms like "painful" and "grievous"? (verse 23)

4 Solomon made a major breakthrough in verse 24. What did he discover?

5 In summary, what would Solomon say gives meaning to work?

WRAP-UP:
IN LIGHT OF OUR STUDY IN ECCLESIASTES, EACH MAN SAY WHAT HE THINKS GIVES HIS WORK MEANING.

LET'S PRAY: (SEE PRAYER JOURNAL)

MY RESPONSE AS A PROMISE KEEPER

I will increasingly bring God into my work by _____

_____

I will insure that the value I place on work will not be eroded by my fellow workers by _____

_____

JOHNNY PAYCHECK

FOURTH IN THE SERIES ON THE BIBLICAL BASIS FOR WORK

WARM-UP: SHORTLY BEFORE THE TURN OF THE CENTURY, TWO FRIENDS WERE HIRED ON THE SAME DAY BY THE RAILROAD COMPANY. AFTER A NUMBER OF YEARS, ONE MAN WAS STILL ON THE LABOR CREW, REPAIRING TRACK, WHILE THE OTHER HAD BEEN PROMOTED TO PRESIDENT. WHEN ASKED ABOUT THE DIFFERENCE BY HIS CO-WORKERS, THE FIRST MAN SAID, "I GUESS IT GOES BACK TO THE DAY WE WERE HIRED. I WENT TO WORK FOR AN HOURLY WAGE, BUT HE WENT TO WORK FOR THE RAILROAD."

WHAT'S THE PROBLEM WITH JUST WORKING FOR A PAYCHECK?

BACKGROUND

"What do you do for a living?" That's one of the most common questions we're asked. How we answer tells much about who we are and what our lives are like. Some of us are happy with the answer we give. But many others find it a painful reminder of the treadmill they're on. What does God think about our job? And what would happen if we could see ourselves as a co-worker with God in what we do?

READ

ECCLESIASTES 5:10-20

QUESTIONS FOR INTERACTION:

1 What are some of the benefits of being a hard worker versus a hoarding worker?

2 Many people misjudge money's ability to provide security. Why are some of the richest people the most insecure?

3 What do we learn here about making good investments from our earnings on the job? What if we don't?

4 Do you think God is concerned that we enjoy our work life? Why or why not?

5 What are the blessings of God to us in being able to work day after day over the years?

WRAP-UP: AGREE OR DISAGREE: YOU ARE TO GO TO WORK FOR THE SAME REASON YOU GO TO CHURCH. WHY OR WHY NOT?

 LET'S PRAY: (SEE PRAYER JOURNAL)

MY RESPONSE AS A PROMISE KEEPER

In what ways will my workday change if I see myself as a co-worker with God? _____

_____

I will try going to work this week for the same reason I go to church.

WHO GETS THE GLORY?

FIRST IN THE SERIES ON BIBLICAL QUALITY MANAGEMENT

● ●

WARM-UP: IN TODAY'S ECONOMY, SOME ENGINEERS AND INVENTORS HAVE A SERIOUS STRUGGLE WITH LOYALTY TO THEIR EMPLOYER. A NEW PRODUCT OR A NEW DESIGN THAT THEY PROVIDE COULD GENERATE MILLIONS OF DOLLARS IN ADDITIONAL REVENUE TO THEIR COMPANY. YET AN ARTICLE IN THE BUSINESS SECTION OF THE NEWSPAPER PRAISES THE COMPANY BUT BARELY MENTIONS THE NAMES OF THE INVENTORS.

WHY ARE WE SO CONCERNED THAT THE INVENTORS GET SO LITTLE OF THE GLORY?

BACKGROUND

Our workplace motives sometimes may not be clear to us. Motives can be hidden by the need to get a paycheck or to succeed in a project that will enhance our résumé. Nonetheless, the question of who we're really working for is bound to surface, especially when it comes to giving credit for a job well done. In today's session, the apostle Paul calls us to an incredibly high standard of motive for the marketplace. Our challenge is to make it practical.

READ

1 CORINTHIANS 10:31—11:1

QUESTIONS FOR INTERACTION:

1 What might it mean to "bring glory" to your company?

What comes to mind to define the phrase "to the glory of God"

2 If a worker is not doing his or her work for the glory of God, for whose glory might achievements be? What does this glory look like?

3 Why do you think the apostle made living and working for the glory of God so inclusive (eating, drinking, whatever you do)?

4 What models exist in history or in our day of work being done for the glory of God? What was the impact on the workplace and life?

5 If you were to start working for the glory of God today, what might change?

WRAP-UP: YOU PROBABLY CAN'T "ANNOUNCE" IN YOUR WORKPLACE THAT YOU'RE WORKING FOR THE GLORY OF GOD. TALK TOGETHER OF HOW A FELLOW WORKER MIGHT RECOGNIZE THAT YOUR MOTIVE IS TO GLORIFY GOD.

 LET'S PRAY: (SEE PRAYER JOURNAL)

MY RESPONSE AS A PROMISE KEEPER

What barriers exist in my life to accepting the apostle's challenge to do all for the glory of God? _____

If God gets the glory, what's in it for me? _____

_____

"NO WINE BEFORE ITS TIME"

SECOND IN THE SERIES ON BIBLICAL QUALITY MANAGEMENT

WARM-UP: THE DEMING PRIZE IS ONE OF THE MOST COVETED ANNUAL AWARDS FOR PRODUCT QUALITY AND DEPENDABILITY. UNFORTUNATELY FOR THE UNITED STATES, W. EDWARDS DEMING COULD FIND LITTLE SUPPORT FOR HIS PRINCIPLES OF QUALITY HERE, SO HE MOVED TO JAPAN TO CARRY OUT HIS LIFE'S WORK. DEMING'S PRINCIPLES RADICALLY CHANGED THE AUTOMOTIVE INDUSTRY THERE. DISCUSS TOGETHER WHAT PART QUALITY PLAYS IN YOUR WORKPLACE.

BACKGROUND

The first miracle Jesus performed was intended to authenticate His mission as Messiah. A second look at what He did has much to say to us about the kind of job we're doing. For if God is interested in quality, that's the first reason we should be. That may be some kind of miracle for your workplace!

READ

JOHN 2:1-11

QUESTIONS FOR INTERACTION:

1 The origins of excellence and quality in goods and services may be difficult to trace. Yet we all recognize their presence when we see them. What are some examples from the Originator of quality?

2 Why do you think Jesus created such quality wine at the wedding? He could have gotten by with doing a lot less. In fact, that was the expectation.

WALK ⇨ WORK

PK PROMISE KEEPERS®
MEN OF INTEGRITY

3 What meaning might we attach to the fact that Jesus' first miracle was this one?

4 What effect did the quality work of Jesus have on the wine steward? On the disciples?

WRAP-UP.
EACH MAN RELATE HOW HIS WORKPLACE WITNESS IS AFFECTED BY THE KIND OF WORK HE DOES.

 LET'S PRAY: (SEE PRAYER JOURNAL)

● ●

MY RESPONSE AS A PROMISE KEEPER

What's one way I can introduce quality and excellence into my workplace? _____

_____

What barriers do I anticipate as I begin to implement quality in my work?

_____

_____

CALLED ON THE CARPET

THIRD IN THE SERIES ON BIBLICAL QUALITY MANAGEMENT

• •

WARM-UP: TODD ANTICIPATES BEING HIRED BY HIS FATHER'S COMPANY, WHERE HIS DAD IS THE CEO. ON THE DAY OF THE INTERVIEW, TODD IS CASUALLY DRESSED AND CASUALLY PREPARED. UPON ENTERING THE ROOM, HE IS GREETED BY A TEAM OF SHARPLY DRESSED MEN AND WOMEN—READY TO TEST TODD'S QUALIFICATIONS FOR THE PROPOSED JOB. TALK TOGETHER ABOUT WHAT WRONG ASSUMPTIONS TODD MAY HAVE MADE ABOUT HIS FATHER AND HIS COMPANY.

BACKGROUND

Israel's history includes a period when the priests made some wrong assumptions about God and the standards of quality service He expected. The quality of their work became so casual that the Lord had to speak out against them through the prophet Malachi. But can we really say God is interested in the quality of work we do? This is part of our discovery in today's session as we seek to apply the timeless Word to our lives.

READ

MALACHI 1:6—2:3

QUESTIONS FOR INTERACTION:

1 In Malachi's day, quality service in the priesthood was a problem. What was wrong? How did this affect the work they did?

2 Why in the world would the priests not realize there was a problem with the quality of their work?

3 In the work of priests, what was a quality job intended to look like?

4 Why do you think the Lord was so troubled by the loss of quality work among His priests?

5 What happens to the worker when his work is of poor quality? What happens when there is good-quality work? (see Proverbs 22:29)

WRAP-UP. AGREE OR DISAGREE: MY FELLOW WORKERS OFTEN EXPECT A BETTER JOB FROM ME IF THEY KNOW I'M A CHRISTIAN. WHY OR WHY NOT?

 LET'S PRAY: (SEE PRAYER JOURNAL)

● ●

MY RESPONSE AS A PROMISE KEEPER

Since the Lord values quality, the first thing I need to do in my work is

_____

_____

FILLED AND SKILLED

FOURTH IN THE SERIES ON BIBLICAL QUALITY MANAGEMENT

• •

WARM-UP: LATE IN HIS CAREER, RUSTY STAUB BECAME A SPECIALIZED PLAYER FOR THE NEW YORK METS. ALTHOUGH HIS FIELDING AND RUNNING SPEED HAD DIMINISHED, HE REMAINED AN EXCELLENT PINCH HITTER. HIS UNIQUE SKILLS WERE MAXIMIZED BY BEING USED ONLY IN THE LATE INNINGS, AND ONLY AGAINST RIGHT-HANDED PITCHERS. WHAT WORKPLACE SKILLS ARE PRESENT IN OUR GROUP MEMBERS?

BACKGROUND

One of the most unusual and inspiring stories in the Old Testament tells how the tabernacle was constructed by the Hebrews. It was a kind of portable temple. The part we're interested in for today's session concerns how God called and enabled the workers for the task. We can profit greatly from learning about this process, for the person who perceives that his or her skills are from the Lord takes a quantum leap in productivity and excellence.

READ

EXODUS 35:30— 36:8

QUESTIONS FOR INTERACTION:

1 Why do you think the Lord was concerned about skilled workers in the construction of the tabernacle? Why was He so concerned about quality?

2 God had an important job to do, where quality was of the essence. What did He do?

3 Sometimes a skilled worker will say God has filled him. What is there about his work that would make us agree?

4 In 35:34, what's the significance of the skilled worker being able to teach others?

WRAP-UP: THERE'S A DIFFERENCE BETWEEN SOMEONE WHO IS SKILLED AND SOMEONE WHO IS <u>FILLED</u> AND SKILLED. TOGETHER COME UP WITH SOME EXAMPLES OF EACH AS YOU HAVE OBSERVED THEM IN THE WORKPLACE.

 LET'S PRAY: (SEE PRAYER JOURNAL)

MY RESPONSE AS A PROMISE KEEPER

What message does shoddy work communicate to my associates? _____

_____

What can I do today to be a worker who demonstrates being filled and skilled? _____

ONE WISH FROM A GENIE

FIRST IN THE SERIES ON ETHICAL DECISION MAKING

● ●

WARM-UP: NUMEROUS STORIES—FROM ALI BABA TO ALADDIN—HAVE PORTRAYED THE EXISTENCE OF A MYSTICAL, MAGICAL LAMP. IF THE LUCKY FINDER CAN RUB THE LAMP AND RELEASE THE GENIE, HE WILL BE GRANTED ANY WISH. WHAT CHILD (OR ADULT) HAS NOT FANTASIZED OF SUCH AN OPPORTUNITY? LOOKING BACK OVER YOUR CHILDHOOD, IF YOU COULD HAVE HAD ONE WISH FROM A GENIE, WHAT MIGHT IT HAVE BEEN?

BACKGROUND

If God were to tell you, "Ask what you wish Me to give you," in preparation for a job requiring discernment and ethical decision making, how would you answer? Today's session helps us understand the core of strong, ethical leadership. Solomon had just been handed the role of leading a nation. His father/mentor had walked closely with God and left huge shoes to fill. God, in preparing this young king, said he could ask for anything.

READ

1 KINGS 3:3-15

QUESTIONS FOR INTERACTION:

1 "Solomon showed his love for the Lord" are the opening words of our biblical paragraph. What may be some reasons for his strong faith?

2 Why do you think the Lord was eager to offer this new king a gift of any description?

MEN OF INTEGRITY

56

3 How might we explain the amazing humility of the new king?

4 How would the gift of God help Solomon in ethical decision making?

5 For some reason, the Lord also gave the new king everything we might have expected Solomon to request. Why the bonus?

WRAP-UP.
NOW THAT YOU'VE COMPLETED THIS STUDY, HOW WOULD YOU ANSWER GOD IF HE TOLD YOU, "ASK WHAT YOU WISH ME TO GIVE YOU"?

LET'S PRAY: (SEE PRAYER JOURNAL)

MY RESPONSE AS A PROMISE KEEPER

What decision or situation am I facing where I need the wisdom of God?

_____

In view of today's study, what should I do? _____

_____

A Bad Day at the Realtor's Office

Second in the Series on Ethical Decision Making

●●

Warm-Up:

A TRUSTED GOVERNMENT FIGURE MISUSES THE POWER OF HIS OFFICE, AS WELL AS PUBLIC FUNDS, AND THE FACTS ARE BROUGHT TO LIGHT. WHAT IMPACT DOES THAT HAVE ON THE WHOLE RELATIONSHIP BETWEEN THE GOVERNMENT AND THE PEOPLE IT IS SUPPOSED TO BE SERVING?

BACKGROUND

Trying to define what it means to be honest may seem easy. We all know what honesty is. Yet it's a lot harder to really live that way. Our circumstances try to tell us it's impossible to be fully honest in all situations. Today's session will look at a couple in a business deal who, through their rationalizations, were less than completely honest. And their deceptive act cost them their lives. Let's discover what went wrong.

READ

ACTS 4:32—5:13

Questions for Interaction:

1 When you think back on your previous business deals, which one makes you cringe a little? Why?

2 What do you think motivated Ananias and Sapphira to sell some of their property and give the money to the church?

3 What made this outwardly charitable act dishonest? How could they have done this?

CONSIDER THIS:

SIGN POSTED INSIDE A COLLEGE-TOWN SUPER-MARKET: "WE MAY BE THE FRIENDLIEST SUPERMAR-KET IN TOWN, BUT WE *WILL* PROSECUTE SHOPLIFTERS."

4 As the couple were putting their plan together, how do you think they would have defined *honesty?*

5 According to the apostle Peter, what was the root problem in the couple's scheme?

WRAP-UP: DESCRIBE A TIME WHEN SOMEONE YOU KNOW WAS DISHONEST OR DECEPTIVE. (NO NAMES, PLEASE.) WHERE DID IT LEAD? WHAT DID IT COST HIM? WHAT DID YOU LEARN?

LET'S PRAY: (SEE PRAYER JOURNAL)

MY RESPONSE AS A PROMISE KEEPER

What's in it for me if I'm honest? _____

_____

What's in it for me if I'm not honest? _____

_____

When I'm not honest, who is affected? _____

_____

THE FUDGE FACTOR

THIRD IN THE SERIES ON ETHICAL DECISION MAKING

WARM-UP: TAXES. THAT SINGLE WORD GENERATES A REACTION FROM EVERYONE. COMEDIAN STEVE MARTIN HAS SUGGESTED (TONGUE IN CHEEK) THAT YOU COULD MAKE A MILLION DOLLARS AND YET PAY NO TAXES BY SIMPLY MEMORIZING TWO WORDS—"I FORGOT!" ALTHOUGH IT'S NO LAUGHING MATTER, INCOME-TAX CHEATING AND TAX AVOIDANCE HAVE BECOME MAJOR THREATS TO ANY HOPE OF A BALANCED BUDGET. WHY IS IT SUCH A COMMON TEMPTATION TO INTENTIONALLY DECEIVE THE IRS?

BACKGROUND

Making the right decision usually just calls for obedience—we know what we need to do. But obeying isn't necessarily easy. It may set in motion all kinds of ramifications we don't want to face. Israel's first king, Saul, was in such a situation. He was to be God's instrument of justice on the oppressive Amalekites. Today's session takes a close look at his struggle—and maybe ours—to simply make the right choice.

READ

 ## 1 SAMUEL 15:1-24

QUESTIONS FOR INTERACTION:

1 In our day, we can't conceive of exterminating a tribe of people. Yet Saul was given the command to do just that. Why do you think he did so without hesitation?

2 The king attacked and conquered the enemy! Or did he? In his own mind, how well do you think he carried out his orders?

WALK ⇒ WORK

PK PROMISE KEEPERS®
MEN OF INTEGRITY

3 The king felt trapped between the command of God and the will of the people. What counsel would you have given him to resolve this dilemma?

4 Why was Saul able to rationalize his choice as *obedience* to God?

5 How did Saul define *obedience?* How does God define *obedience?*

WRAP-UP: DECISIONS DO HAVE CONSEQUENCES. RECALL A DECISION THAT BURDENED SOMEONE YOU KNOW WITH SERIOUS CONSEQUENCES. (NO NAMES, PLEASE.)

 LET'S PRAY: (SEE PRAYER JOURNAL)

• •

MY RESPONSE AS A PROMISE KEEPER

What are some decisions in my workplace this week that will simply call for obedience? _____

_____

If there's a struggle with some of them, what makes it difficult? _____

_____

"So, What's the Big Deal?"

FOURTH IN THE SERIES ON ETHICAL DECISION MAKING

● ●

WARM-UP:

BRUCE IS A PURCHASING MANAGER FOR A LARGE CORPORATION. A FEW YEARS AGO, HE WAS FACED WITH A DILEMMA WHEN AWARDING A LARGE CONTRACT. ONE OF THE BIDDING COMPANIES TRIED TO SWEETEN ITS DEAL BY OFFERING HIM TWO PERSONAL GIFTS—A VACATION AT A COMPANY-OWNED RESORT AND A NEW FISHING BOAT IN HIS DRIVEWAY. BRUCE'S FAVORITE HOBBY IS FISHING. WHAT ETHICAL ISSUES WERE AT STAKE HERE FOR BOTH BRUCE AND HIS COMPANY?

BACKGROUND

Taking things that don't belong to us and padding accounts are common in the workplace. And the things or money taken aren't usually considered stolen by those who do it. Rather, they rationalize that they're making up for low wages, poor working conditions, or whatever. But surely there's an effect on us when we steal. In today's session, we'll meet a man who padded his account and thought, "So, what's the big deal?"

READ

2 KINGS 5:1-27

QUESTIONS FOR INTERACTION:

1 Deep gratitude for his miraculous healing motivated Naaman to lavish gifts on the prophet Elisha. Yet they were refused. Why do you think Elisha just said no?

2 The opportunity to gain something from the grateful Syrian was overwhelming to Gehazi. How might he have rationalized his devious strategy?

3 Why do you think Gehazi could state an outright lie so matter-of-factly to Elisha, the man of God? What do we learn about the art of lying here?

4 What were the dreadful consequences of Gehazi's decision to pad his account before his master?

5 Why didn't Elisha just forgive Gehazi?

WRAP-UP: "IT'S JUST NOT THAT BIG A DEAL!" WHAT ARE SOME LITTLE THINGS THAT ARE DONE SO EASILY—INFLATING A REPORT, TAKING HOME PENS AND PAPER CLIPS—THAT CIRCUMVENT THE LORD'S PROVISION?

 LET'S PRAY: (SEE PRAYER JOURNAL)

● ●

MY RESPONSE AS A PROMISE KEEPER

What are some *little things* in my work life that may need my attention?

_____

How can the principle of 1 Corinthians 11:31 be applied to my workplace ethics? _____

TAKE THAT!

FIRST IN THE SERIES ON BUILDING WORKPLACE RELATIONSHIPS

● ●

WARM-UP: MARTIN LUTHER KING JR. WAS A GREAT HERO OF THE TWENTIETH CENTURY. PERHAPS IT WAS BECAUSE HE KNEW HOW TO RESPOND TO INSULT AND INJURY. "WHEN EVIL MEN PLOT, GOOD MEN MUST PLAN," HE SAID. "WHEN EVIL MEN BURN AND BOMB, GOOD MEN MUST BUILD AND BIND. WHEN EVIL MEN SHOUT UGLY WORDS OF HATRED, GOOD MEN MUST COMMIT THEMSELVES TO THE GLORIES OF LOVE." WHY DOES "EVIL FOR EVIL" COME SO NATURALLY? HOW DOES REACTING THAT WAY AFFECT WORKPLACE RELATIONSHIPS?

BACKGROUND

Sooner or later, workplace relationships will mean conflict. When someone offends us or misrepresents us, what are we to do? The world's answer is easy: Get even. But if we're growing in the Lord, we'll be uneasy with that response. We know we're called to do better. Today's session outlines a revolutionary plan. It may take a few conflicts to get it right, but when we do, it will be a new day at our workplace.

READ

1 PETER 3:8-12

QUESTIONS FOR INTERACTION:

1 What character qualities would you say are essential for relationships to flourish? Why do you think Peter selected the five qualities mentioned in verse 8?

2 What's the alternative response if we don't return evil for evil? How would reacting this way affect workplace relationships?

PROMISE
KEEPERS®
MEN OF INTEGRITY

64

3 Why should we be interested in giving a blessing to someone who has done evil to us?

4 Peter brought in a psalm (verses 10-12) to describe the blessing response. Discuss the steps he explained.

WRAP-UP: YOU'VE HAD A FALLING-OUT WITH A CO-WORKER BECAUSE HE CRITICIZED YOU ON A PROJECT REPORT. APART FROM SETTING THE RECORD STRAIGHT, YOU WANT TO MEND THE RELATIONSHIP. DISCUSS HOW YOU COULD RESPOND TO HIS INSULT WITH A BLESSING.

 LET'S PRAY: (SEE PRAYER JOURNAL)

MY RESPONSE AS A PROMISE KEEPER

How do I normally try to resolve conflict? _____

_____

How will I be different as a result of applying today's insights? _____

_____

What blessings can I anticipate if I implement this biblical plan for resolving conflict? _____

_____

"GET OUT OF MY FACE!"

SECOND IN THE SERIES ON BUILDING WORKPLACE RELATIONSHIPS

• •

WARM-UP: SKIP HAS REPEATEDLY PUT HIS FAMILY IN JEOPARDY BECAUSE HE WON'T SUBMIT TO AUTHORITY. HE HAS BEEN FIRED FROM FOUR JOBS BECAUSE HE THINKS HE'S ALWAYS RIGHT AND EVERYONE ELSE IS ALWAYS WRONG. UNFORTUNATELY, THE LAST TIME HE WAS FIRED, HE LOST HIS MEDICAL INSURANCE. THREE WEEKS LATER, HIS YOUNG SON WAS DIAGNOSED WITH A HEART CONDITION. NOW SKIP'S REFUSAL TO SUBMIT TO AUTHORITY HAS BROUGHT TRAGEDY TO HIS FAMILY. WHY IS SUBMISSION TO AUTHORITY USUALLY DIFFICULT FOR MEN?

BACKGROUND

Definition: *re-tal-i-ate* vb: "to repay with an act of the same kind, to return an injury or wrong with revenge." Actually, retaliation is defending ourselves and our rights. In this session, we'll look at an incredible alternative to our natural response of retaliation in workplace relationships.

READ

1 PETER 2:18-25

QUESTIONS FOR INTERACTION:

1 Explain why you think Peter elevated submission as the first response of employees to employers.

2 What might be the reason God values suffering for injustices over retaliation?

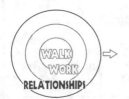

3 How was Jesus able to resist retaliating against His persecutors?

4 What do you suppose would have happened if Jesus had retaliated?

WRAP-UP: HAVE YOUR GROUP GIVE AS MANY EXAMPLES AS THEY CAN (WITHIN YOUR TIME LIMIT) OF CHRISTLIKE RESPONSES TO AUTHORITY.

 LET'S PRAY: (SEE PRAYER JOURNAL)

● ●

MY RESPONSE AS A PROMISE KEEPER

What would happen in my relationship with _____ (co-worker) if I were to respond without retaliation the next time he/she gets in my face? _____

What makes me think I'll really do it? _____

_____

MVP

(MOST VALUABLE PEOPLE)

• •

WARM-UP: LARRY IS A SUCCESSFUL SALESMAN WHO IS AS SMOOTH AS BUTTER. HE LOOKS AT EACH PERSON AS A POTENTIAL CLIENT OR AN OPPORTUNITY TO MAKE MORE MONEY. HE VALUES PEOPLE ONLY FOR WHAT HE CAN GET OUT OF THEM.

HOW COULD YOU COMMUNICATE TO PEOPLE AT WORK THAT THEY HAVE GREAT VALUE TO YOU AS INDIVIDUALS?

BACKGROUND

One clear principle from Scripture is that Jesus valued people. Virtually every page of His life is the record of His concern for others. Not everyone loved Him, but that's often the way it is in real life. Today's session shows how Jesus communicated His regard for people. When we begin to value others, we'll be pleasantly surprised by how we view our workplace in a new way.

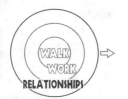

READ

JOHN 1:35-51

QUESTIONS FOR INTERACTION:

1 What was so unusual about John the Baptist's introduction of Jesus that it made John's friends follow Him?

2 We know that building relationships involves time. How did Jesus employ this principle with His new acquaintances?

3 What relationship principles might Jesus have demonstrated that enabled Andrew to know who He really was so quickly?

4 What do you think enticed Philip to accept the invitation of Jesus to enter a special relationship with Him?

CONSIDER THIS:

ON A SIGN LOCATED BY THE TIME CLOCK IN A BUSINESS: "CUSTOMERS ARE NOT INTERRUPTIONS TO OUR BUSY DAY. THEY ARE THE REASON WE GET A PAYCHECK."

5 Nathanael was naturally skeptical about Jesus, yet Jesus still valued him. How did He communicate this? (Note: Nathanael's skepticism of Jesus in John 1:46 likely came from what he knew about Nazareth. It was in an area where as many as seven pagan deities were worshiped. It was, therefore, looked upon with disgust by proper Judean Jews and was second only to Samaria in ill repute.)

WRAP-UP: JESUS DEMONSTRATED THAT RELATIONSHIPS FLOURISH WHEN WE VALUE PEOPLE, SPEND TIME WITH THEM, AND ALLOW SELF-DISCLOSURE. DISCUSS HOW OUR FELLOW WORKERS WOULD KNOW WE VALUE THEM.

 LET'S PRAY: (SEE PRAYER JOURNAL)

• •

MY RESPONSE AS A PROMISE KEEPER

With which people at work do I have the best relationships? How did this happen? _____

Between valuing people, spending time with them, and allowing self-disclosure, which one needs my greatest attention? Why? _____

_____

LOVE AT FIRST SIGHT

● ●

WARM-UP: FRANK IS AN UNUSUAL GUY IN HIS WORKPLACE. HE OFTEN SAYS "I'LL BUY" AT THE BREAKS. HE HAS EVEN BEEN KNOWN TO SHOW INTEREST IN THE FAMILIES OF HIS CO-WORKERS. WHY ARE SOME PEOPLE NATURALLY SUSPICIOUS OF WORKPLACE FRIENDLINESS?

BACKGROUND

Workplace relationships are often difficult to build. Time to talk is limited, many people see the workplace only as a place to work, and we're naturally suspicious of anyone who thinks work is a place for friendships. We ask ourselves, "What are his or her motives?" Nonetheless, Jesus is concerned that we represent Him well at work, and that there is love at first sight among our brothers. That's at the heart of our session today.

READ

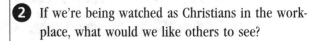

JOHN 13:34-35
AND 15:12-17

QUESTIONS FOR INTERACTION:

1 What relationship principles did Jesus describe for His disciples that enabled them to have distinctive workplace relationships?

2 If we're being watched as Christians in the workplace, what would we like others to see?

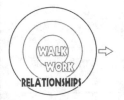

3 How does Jesus want us to be known in the workplace?

4 What does damage to this reputation?

5 What's the reason for initiative on our part in relationships?

WRAP-UP: IF WE DON'T HAVE RELATIONSHIPS WITH CHRISTIANS, HOW WILL WE EVER HAVE RELATIONSHIPS WITH NON-CHRISTIANS? LOOK AGAIN AT JOHN 13:35. DISCUSS TOGETHER: WHERE DOES REACHING OUT TO OTHERS REALLY BEGIN? WHERE HAVE YOU SEEN THIS HAPPEN?

 LET'S PRAY: (SEE PRAYER JOURNAL)

● ●

MY RESPONSE AS A PROMISE KEEPER

What have been two or three of my barriers to being a loving person at work? _____

How will I start overcoming one of them tomorrow? _____

_____

CRASH!

WARM-UP: SOME SURVEYS SUGGEST THAT 6 OUT OF 10 MEN WILL HAVE AT LEAST ONE AFFAIR IN THEIR LIFETIME. THIS HAPPENS IN SPITE OF THE WARNINGS OF DESTRUCTION THAT AN AFFAIR CAN BRING TO A MAN'S LIFE AND HOME. AN AFFAIR OFTEN BEGINS WITH A LUSTFUL THOUGHT OR A FEW ENTICING WORDS SPOKEN BETWEEN CO-WORKERS. LUST COMES TO ALL OF US AT SOME TIME. WHAT'S THE SOURCE OF THIS ALLURING FORCE? HOW DOES IT GET INTO OUR LIVES?

BACKGROUND

What first appeared as an exciting opportunity turned into one of the darkest events of King David's life. He said yes to the lust in his heart, committed adultery, then had the woman's husband killed in an attempted cover-up. His choices profoundly affected his home, his workplace, and his work life. Let's consider what we can do when powerful sexual urges rush in to overtake us.

READ

2 SAMUEL 11:1-15, 26—12:10

QUESTIONS FOR INTERACTION:

1 How might we describe David's situation that made him vulnerable to lust in his heart?

2 King David may have reminisced over the weeks about his thrilling experience. Why might he have thought he would get away with it?

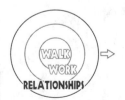

3 How did his lust and cover-up affect his workplace relationships?

4 "Marriage should be honored by all, and the marriage bed kept pure, for God will judge the adulterer and all the sexually immoral" (Hebrews 13:4). Why do you think God Himself takes responsibility to bring to judgment those who live immorally?

WRAP-UP. DISCUSS TOGETHER WHAT MIGHT BE SOME WAYS WE CAN GUARD OURSELVES FROM AN AFFAIR.

 LET'S PRAY: (SEE PRAYER JOURNAL)

MY RESPONSE AS A PROMISE KEEPER

I will recognize with new alertness the deadly potential of lust in me. I will pray for God's protection.

When I sense lust rushing in, I will run to 1 Corinthians 6:18-20 for perspective.

POWER DRIVE

● ●

WARM-UP:

JEFF AND JIM HAVE WORKED TOGETHER ON A CONSTRUCTION CREW FOR ABOUT THREE YEARS. JEFF HAS OBSERVED LATELY THAT HIS PARTNER LOOKS FOR WAYS TO SHOW OFF HIS WORK—HE EVEN TRIES TO SIT NEAR THEIR BOSS AT LUNCH. JIM IS MORE THAN EAGER TO VOLUNTEER FOR EXTRA RESPONSIBILITIES THE BOSS WILL NOTICE. IF A FELLOW WORKER IS DESCRIBED AS BEING ON A POWER TRIP, WHAT IS BEING SAID ABOUT HIM? WHY IS THE LOVE OF POWER A BARRIER TO GOOD WORKPLACE RELATIONSHIPS?

BACKGROUND

The two faces of ambition are often difficult to differentiate. Is ambition simply energy for the job or a quest for power and control? When it's a drive for power, it becomes a high barrier to relationships. Even the 12 disciples of Jesus had to face a day when ambition raised its two heads. In today's session, we'll see the skill of Jesus in handling the sharp curves of someone on a power drive.

READ

MATTHEW 20:20-28

QUESTIONS FOR INTERACTION:

1 What does Mom really want for her boys in today's passage? What do the three of them hope to gain from their positions of power?

2 How did Jesus respond to this power play? Which face of ambition do you think He saw?

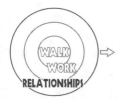

PROMISE
KEEPERS®
MEN OF INTEGRITY

3 In what ways did this power drive become a barrier to good relationships?

4 What is Jesus' plan for influence and power among fellow workers?

WRAP-UP:
DISCUSS TOGETHER WHY MOST PEOPLE WOULD THINK JESUS' PLAN TO BE UNWORKABLE IN TODAY'S BUSINESS COMMUNITY.

 LET'S PRAY: (SEE PRAYER JOURNAL)

• •

MY RESPONSE AS A PROMISE KEEPER

If I desire more godly power and influence in my workplace, my first step is to _____

I will build a bridge of relationship with _____ through serving him/her, not seeking to rule.

THE CREED OF GREED

THIRD IN THE SERIES ON BARRIERS TO WORKPLACE RELATIONSHIPS

• •

WARM-UP: RICHARD WAGNER TOLD A GREAT STORY IN HIS OPERA "THE RING." A DRAGON LIVED IN A CAVE AND GUARDED A GREAT TREASURE OF GOLD. HE SPENT HIS ENTIRE EXISTENCE SITTING IN THAT DARK CAVE, LOOKING OUT ON A BEAUTIFUL, LUSH FOREST THAT HE NEVER ENJOYED. MANY MEN LIVE THAT WAY. THEY SPEND THEIR DAYS GREEDILY GUARDING AND ADDING TO A TREASURE THAT WILL SOON FADE AWAY. AS A RESULT, THEY NEVER REALLY EXPERIENCE CONTENTMENT IN THEIR MARRIAGE, CHILDREN, FRIENDSHIPS, OR WORKPLACE. WHY DO YOU THINK CONTENTMENT IS SUCH A RARE TRAIT? DEFINE CONTENTMENT BY DESCRIBING SOME CONTENTED PEOPLE YOU KNOW.

BACKGROUND

Few attitudes erect a higher barrier to relationships than greed. In fact, many people believe it's the number-one cause of the world's problems. The greed barrier isn't just a result of our materialistic times, either. Jesus stated what really fills the greedy heart. That will be one of our discoveries today as we consider a man who lived by the creed of greed. Interestingly, no mention is made of his having any friends.

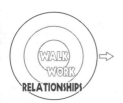

READ

LUKE 12:13-21

QUESTIONS FOR INTERACTION:

1 Jesus had a problem with the opening statement made in our text for today. Why do you think it brought a negative reaction from Him?

2 In the story Jesus told to illustrate His point, why do you think the rich farmer was so vulnerable to greed's grip?

3 Agree or disagree, and spell out why: A poor farmer would not have been vulnerable to greed.

4 How might we explain the absence of any mention of the man's friends or family?

WRAP-UP. HOW HAVE YOU SEEN GREED BECOME A BARRIER TO RELATIONSHIPS? ON THE OTHER HAND, WHAT DO YOU THINK CONTENTMENT DOES TO RELATIONSHIPS? DISCUSS TOGETHER.

 LET'S PRAY: (SEE PRAYER JOURNAL)

• •

MY RESPONSE AS A PROMISE KEEPER

It's unthinkable that I would subscribe to the creed of greed. Yet, what evidence might there be of it in my use of money? _____

_____

This week, I will carry a Post-it note on my credit card with these words from Luke 12:15 (NASB):

> "For not even when one has an abundance does his life consist of his possessions." Jesus

LOOKING DOWN YOUR NOSE

FOURTH IN THE SERIES ON BARRIERS TO WORKPLACE RELATIONSHIPS

• •

WARM-UP: AT THE ANNUAL COMPANY GOLF OUTING, MIKE, WHO WORKED IN THE MAIL-ROOM, FOUND HIMSELF WITH AN INTERESTING FOURSOME. HE WAS TEAMED WITH THE COMPANY ACCOUNTANT, CORPORATE ATTORNEY, AND THE CEO. ON THE FIFTH TEE, THE CEO COMMENTED TO THE ATTORNEY, "WHO IS IN CHARGE OF THESE PAIRINGS?"
WHY IS IT THAT WE OFTEN CAN'T ACCEPT AND LIVE WITH PEOPLE WHO ARE DIFFERENT FROM US?

BACKGROUND

Looking down on another person or group likely goes back to the beginning of civilization. Why can't we accept and live with people who are different? When such attitudes invade the workplace, it can be painful and even ugly. After so many centuries of caste-thinking, what can we say to turn this around? Fresh words of hope come from our study today.

READ

LUKE 7:36-50

QUESTIONS FOR INTERACTION:

1 The caste system isn't limited to India; it's present in every workplace. What form does it take where we work?

2 Why might the host of the dinner Jesus attended be so judgmental toward the woman who slipped in uninvited?

3 Jesus confronted the attitude of His host who had no problem with looking down on another person or class. What did He say is at the heart of such thinking?

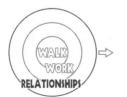

4 How could Jesus have been so accepting of the woman?

CONSIDER THIS:

"IT IS NEVER TOO LATE
TO GIVE UP YOUR
PREJUDICES."

HENRY DAVID THOREAU

How might the woman have felt after Jesus' story?

5 If the host, a Pharisee, were ever to put an end to his biased thinking, what would he have to do?

WRAP-UP: DISCUSS SOME REASONS PEOPLE GET LOOKED DOWN UPON (E.G., EDUCATION, ACCENT, STYLE OF CLOTHES). WHAT DO THOSE PEOPLE OFTEN HEAR FROM US IN THE WORKPLACE?

 LET'S PRAY: (SEE PRAYER JOURNAL)

● ●

MY RESPONSE AS A PROMISE KEEPER

With what group of people or individuals am I thoughtlessly judgmental?

_____

How might I be hurting them? _____

_____

I will begin today to go out of my way to include the excluded in my life.

WE FIX FLATS

WARM-UP: AS RALPH DROVE ACROSS THE NEW BRIDGE, HE MARVELED AT THE WAY IT REDUCED TRAFFIC CONGESTION AND SHAVED 20 MINUTES OFF HIS MORNING COMMUTE. HE FOUND HIMSELF WISHING IT HAD BEEN BUILT YEARS BEFORE. BUT BUILDING BRIDGES BETWEEN PEOPLE MAKES AN EVEN GREATER IMPACT IN THE LIFE OF OUR COUNTRY AND OUR WORLD. SOMETIMES WE CAN BUILD BRIDGES TO NEW RELATIONSHIPS, AND OFTEN WE NEED TO REBUILD THE BRIDGE OF AN EXISTING RELATIONSHIP. DISCUSS TOGETHER: IN OUR WORK-PLACE EXPERIENCE, WHAT HAVE BEEN SOME OF THE CAUSES OF BROKEN RELATIONSHIPS? WHAT HAVE WE SEEN WORK TO FIX THEM?

BACKGROUND

Today's session is about the broken relationship between two brothers, Jacob and Esau. Separated not only by time but also by fear, what would it take to bring them back together? We'll discover today what each of them did to fix their shattered relationship.

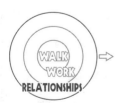

READ

GENESIS 27:30-38, 41-42; 32:3-13

QUESTIONS FOR INTERACTION:

1 What caused the break between Jacob and Esau? Why was a quick and easy fix not likely?

deception:

2 What do you think each brother considered doing about their relationship? What did they finally decide separately to do as a settlement?

3 The day finally came when they would have to face each other again. Read the rest of the story in Genesis 33:1-11. What do you think was each man's hope for mending the broken relationship?

CONSIDER THIS:

THE LONGER YOU CARRY A GRUDGE, THE HEAVIER IT GETS.

CHINESE PROVERB

4 How did this relationship between Jacob and Esau get "fixed"?

WRAP-UP.

LIST AND DISCUSS THREE OR FOUR PRINCIPLES FOR MENDING BROKEN RELATIONSHIPS WE DISCOVERED IN TODAY'S STORY.

 LET'S PRAY: (SEE PRAYER JOURNAL)

MY RESPONSE AS A PROMISE KEEPER

I will begin to seek God's help for repairing the broken relationship I have with _____.

One of the first things I know I must do in fixing this relationship is to

_____

BUSY SIGNAL

SECOND IN THE SERIES ON
BRIDGE-BUILDING RELATIONSHIPS

• •

WARM-UP: FOR SOME REASON, KEN SEES OTHERS AS INTERRUPTIONS OF HIS PLANS, AND HE DOESN'T TRY VERY HARD TO CONCEAL IT. CONSEQUENTLY, IN MEETINGS, PASSING HIM IN THE HALL, OR EVEN AT CHURCH, NO ONE FEELS GOOD ABOUT TALKING WITH HIM. DISCUSS TOGETHER THE VARIOUS THINGS THAT TEND TO MAKE US LOOK AT PEOPLE AS INTERRUPTIONS.

BACKGROUND

The pace of modern life has hit us so hard that we're unaware of how our perspective on people has been affected. Do we see them as interruptions in our busy day or as invitations to serve, to care for, and to know? Many avoid this question by saying they'll think about it when things slow down. Today's session covers a day in the life of a busy person. Let's look for the ways He built bridges of relationships.

READ

MARK 1:29-39;
2:1-2

QUESTIONS FOR INTERACTION:

1 What do you think helped Jesus see people as invitations, not interruptions?

2 What relationship bridges did Jesus build so that He and the people could connect?

3 What kinds of things was Jesus able to offer people that we can offer as well?

CONSIDER THIS:

FOUR DOORS TO CONVERSATION WITH BUSY PEOPLE:

DOOR 1
  BUSINESS SUCCESS
DOOR 2
  BUSINESS FAILURE
DOOR 3
  MARRIAGE
DOOR 4
  FAMILY

4 People can easily drain the life out of us. How did Jesus meet that challenge?

WRAP-UP: DISCUSS WHAT IT WILL TAKE FOR US TO SEE PEOPLE AS JESUS DID—AS INVITATIONS RATHER THAN INTERRUPTIONS.

 LET'S PRAY: (SEE PRAYER JOURNAL)

● ●

MY RESPONSE AS A PROMISE KEEPER

It's easy to feel too busy to relate to the people around me at work. The first thing I need to do to start building more, or better, bridges is to

_____

_____

WHEN IN ROME . . .

THIRD IN THE SERIES ON
BRIDGE-BUILDING RELATIONSHIPS

WARM-UP: AFTER A LONG, HOT DAY ON THE JOB, DAN WAS INVITED BY HIS FELLOW WORKERS TO JOIN THEM FOR A "COLD ONE" AT MURPHY'S BAR. DAN QUICKLY RESPONDED WITH, "OH, I ALREADY HAVE PLANS!" IN REALITY, HE FEARED LOSING HIS TESTIMONY WITH THEM. IF DAN WENT WITH HIS CO-WORKERS, WOULD HE BE COMPROMISING HIS STANDARDS OF "BECOMING ALL THINGS TO ALL MEN"?

BACKGROUND

A benefit of growing up in one area and staying there most of your life is that you know just about everyone, and everyone seems to know you. But our culture is highly mobile, and many people never even meet their neighbors. Climbing into another person's world helps us to know what his life is like. This is vital in building relationships. Today's session applies this relationship principle to the workplace.

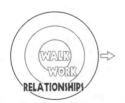

READ

1 CORINTHIANS 9:19-23

(Use the *Living Bible* if possible.)

QUESTIONS FOR INTERACTION:

1 What's necessary to connect with people *different* from us if we hope to have a relationship with them?

2 Why would anyone want to build a bridge with someone beyond cultural or racial barriers? (see verse 19)

3 If we could meet Paul the apostle and have an unhurried hour with him, what might impress us about him?

4 How would you describe Paul's *motivation* for making relationships across such a broad spectrum?

5 What keeps most of us safely in our comfort zones, not reaching out to new relationships around us?

WRAP-UP: WHAT KINDS OF PEOPLE AROUND YOU WILL YOU NEVER CONNECT TO NATU-RALLY? WHAT MIGHT CHANGE THIS FORECAST?

 LET'S PRAY: (SEE PRAYER JOURNAL)

MY RESPONSE AS A PROMISE KEEPER

I will identify the people at work who are outside my comfort zone and begin to look for opportunities to meet them and learn their names.

I will begin to pray for and learn about one of the affinity groups near me with whom bridges of relationship might be built.

THE TREE'D MUSKETEER

FOURTH IN THE SERIES ON
BRIDGE-BUILDING RELATIONSHIPS

● ●

WARM-UP: IN A SMALL FARMING COMMUNITY, TWO MEN HAVE PUT TOGETHER A BI-WEEKLY OUTREACH BREAKFAST. OVER THE LAST COUPLE OF MONTHS, DENNIS AND ROGER HAVE OBSERVED THAT THERE ARE NO NON-CHRISTIANS IN ATTENDANCE. DISCUSS TOGETHER HOW THEY MIGHT DO A BETTER JOB OF CONNECTING TO THOSE THEY DESIRE TO REACH FOR CHRIST.

BACKGROUND

Building bridges to the people around us is a challenge, especially when we would like to introduce them to Jesus. Where do we begin? And how do we know they're interested in the first place? Let's look closely at how the Master of bridge building related to someone who was unpopular and clearly not yet one of His followers.

READ

LUKE 19:1-10

QUESTIONS FOR INTERACTION:

❶ What makes building bridges to non-Christians challenging for many of us?

❷ Why might it have been highly unlikely that Jesus would ever talk to Zacchaeus on His way to Jerusalem?

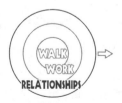

WALK
WORK
RELATIONSHIPS

3 What were some of the indicators that Zacchaeus wanted to get to know Jesus?

4 What was the relationship bridge Jesus built to cross over to this unlikely friend? What made it so effective?

WRAP-UP: WHAT ARE SOME OF THE RISKS YOU FACE IF YOU ATTEMPT TO BUILD BRIDGES TO NON-CHRISTIANS IN YOUR WORKPLACE? HOW DID JESUS ASSURE HIS GRUMBLING FRIENDS THAT THE RISKS OF GETTING TO KNOW ZACCHAEUS WERE WORTH TAKING?

 LET'S PRAY: (SEE PRAYER JOURNAL)

MY RESPONSE AS A PROMISE KEEPER

I will seek the necessary training to be able to talk to the Zacchaeus types in my workplace.

I will tell the Lord I'm available to become one of His bridge builders.

"BEAM ME UP, SCOTTY!"

FIRST IN THE SERIES ON MOTIVATION FOR WORKPLACE MINISTRY

● ●

WARM-UP: ON A BUSINESS TRIP, PETE NOTICED THAT THE MAN SEATED NEXT TO HIM ON THE PLANE WAS READING THE EASTER ISSUE OF TIME MAGAZINE. PETE WONDERED IF GOD MIGHT BE GIVING HIM AN OPPORTUNITY TO SHARE HIS FAITH IN JESUS CHRIST. HOW MIGHT PETE OPEN A CONVERSATION ABOUT SPIRITUAL THINGS? (NOTE: PLAN TO SPEND AT LEAST 10 MINUTES ON TODAY'S WARM-UP.)

BACKGROUND

Each day around the world, countless people serve others for the good of humanity. Yet one of the amazing realities of life is that Almighty God gives us opportunities to serve Him in helping others discover new life in Jesus. Today's session is the story of one man who demonstrated what God can do when we're available to Him. Science fiction action pales next to the real-life drama of today's story of Philip.

READ

ACTS 8:26-40

QUESTIONS FOR INTERACTION:

(Use no more than 20 minutes for these four questions, saving as much time as possible for the wrap-up.)

1 What were some of the preparations by the Holy Spirit for the desert rendezvous? Why might the Spirit make such detailed arrangements?

2 What were three or four ways Philip served (had a ministry to) the Ethiopian?

3 How might we explain the absence of such dramatic events in our lives?

4 What contributes to the kind of thinking that would suggest, "God doesn't work today as He did in Philip's day"?

WRAP-UP: AS MANY OF THE GROUP AS TIME PERMITS, BRIEFLY TELL YOUR OWN STORY OF HOW YOU WERE INTRODUCED TO CHRIST.

 ## LET'S PRAY: (SEE PRAYER JOURNAL)

• •

MY RESPONSE AS A PROMISE KEEPER

Since I don't know how the Lord might desire to use me in serving others, I will tell Him that I'm available today.

I'm impressed with the effectiveness of Philip in his brief time with the Ethiopian. I ask today that the Lord will equip me for such wonderful service.

NIC AT NIGHT

SECOND IN THE SERIES ON MOTIVATION
FOR WORKPLACE MINISTRY

• •

WARM-UP: OVER THE LAST COUPLE OF CENTURIES, AMERICA HAS BEEN KNOWN
AROUND THE WORLD AS A "CHRISTIAN NATION." BUT HOW MANY
AMERICANS KNOW WHAT IT TAKES TO BECOME A REAL CHRISTIAN? BEFORE
WE PROCEED TO A FAMILIAR NEW TESTAMENT ENCOUNTER WITH JESUS,
APPOINT A SCRIBE AND, ALLOWING FIVE MINUTES, TOGETHER LIST WHAT
THINGS A PERSON MUST KNOW IN ORDER TO BECOME A CHRISTIAN.

BACKGROUND

Jesus' impact reached
even the religious leaders
of His day. But any such
leader would have to be
careful in expressing interest in Him and His mes-
sage. In today's session,
we'll glimpse a familiar
face that came to Jesus
in the night hours.

READ

JOHN 3:1-17

QUESTIONS FOR INTERACTION:

1 There's a distinct rise in interest these days in various religious experiences (e.g., crystals, Eastern
meditation, New Age seminars). What might be
some causes for this interest?

2 What do you suppose led Nicodemus to seek an
interview with Jesus?

WALK
WORK
RELATIONSHIPS
MINISTRY

PK PROMISE
KEEPERS®
MEN OF INTEGRITY

3 Some would say (Nicodemus included) that the answer Jesus gave to the question of eternal life was far too simple. What do you think? Why?

4 Since the gospel is so simple (not simplistic), why did Nicodemus have such a hard time figuring it out?

5 If the gospel is so simple, why aren't more people around us becoming Christians?

WRAP-UP: GO BACK TO THE LIST CREATED IN THE WARM-UP SECTION. EACH PERSON IDENTIFY ONE OR TWO ELEMENTS FROM THE LIST THAT ATTRACTED YOU TO JESUS CHRIST.

LET'S PRAY: (SEE PRAYER JOURNAL)

● ●

MY RESPONSE AS A PROMISE KEEPER

A person like Nicodemus may approach me one of these days. I must get ready for him by _____

_____

LOST AND FOUND

THIRD IN THE SERIES ON MOTIVATION FOR WORKPLACE MINISTRY

WARM-UP: THE RED FEATHER LAKES AREA OF THE NORTHERN COLORADO MOUNTAINS IS A FAVORITE PLACE FOR HIKERS, CAMPERS, AND PICNICKERS. WHEN A THREE-YEAR-OLD BOY SEEMINGLY DISAPPEARED FROM HIS FAMILY'S CAMPSITE ONE DAY, NEARLY THE ENTIRE CITY OF NEARBY FORT COLLINS JOINED THE SEARCH. ALL AFTERNOON AND INTO THE NIGHT, THEY LOOKED FOR THE LOST CHILD. NOT UNTIL ALMOST 24 HOURS LATER, WHEN THEY FOUND HIS BODY, DID THEY DISCOVER THAT HE HAD WANDERED ONLY 100 FEET FROM HIS PARENTS. MOST OF US CAN RECALL A TIME AS A CHILD, OR EVEN MORE RECENTLY, WHEN WE WERE LOST. DISCUSS TOGETHER WHAT IT'S LIKE TO BE LOST.

BACKGROUND

How we view people usually determines how we treat them. If we see some as losers, we may treat them with contempt. Today, Jesus will give us an eye exam. Do we see as He sees? Will we view people as He does? These can be hard questions. We may need to exchange contempt for compassion.

READ

LUKE 15:1-10

QUESTIONS FOR INTERACTION:

1 Jesus was concerned for all the people who didn't know His Father or the way into the kingdom of God. What kind of support did He receive for this view from those around Him?

2 How did the Pharisees and scribes see people? How did Jesus see people? Why do you think He saw them differently?

WALK
WORK
RELATIONSHIPS
MINISTRY

PROMISE
KEEPERS®
MEN OF INTEGRITY

92

3 Why do you think heaven gets so excited over a lost person finding Christ?

4 Jesus told three stories about things lost and found—a sheep, a coin, and a son (Luke 15:11-32). Why wasn't one story enough?

WRAP-UP:

THERE MAY BE SOMEONE IN YOUR BUSINESS LIFE WHOM YOU'VE BEEN REJECTING. COULD IT BE THAT HE OR SHE IS JUST LOST? GO AROUND THE GROUP, AND EACH MAN PRAY FOR THE PERSON HE HAS IN MIND.

 LET'S PRAY: (SEE PRAYER JOURNAL)

MY RESPONSE AS A PROMISE KEEPER

There are lost people all around me. I will identify two and begin praying that God's love will find a way to them—possibly through me.

CARE PACKAGE

FOURTH IN THE SERIES ON MOTIVATION FOR WORKPLACE MINISTRY

. . . .

WARM-UP: PERHAPS YOU'VE MET A SALESPERSON IN THE COURSE OF YOUR WORK WHO YOU SENSE CARES MORE ABOUT THE PITCH AND THE PRODUCT THAN ABOUT YOU AS A POTENTIAL BUYER. WHAT MAKES YOU FEEL THAT WAY?

BACKGROUND

Since the gospel contains such life-changing facts, it's essential that it be communicated accurately. But the love of accuracy has sometimes led to the gospel's being presented with little regard for the audience. In today's session, the apostle Paul gives his view on how the gospel should be delivered. Of course he would agree that accuracy is essential. But there's a need for something more. Let's pray for perception as we begin.

READ

1 THESSALONIANS 2:1-12

QUESTIONS FOR INTERACTION:

1 Paul taught that the gospel is communicated through people. What life-qualities can you find in this text being modeled by Paul?

2 The great apostle spoke of God-given *courage* to declare the gospel (verse 2). Why is declaring the gospel often a call to bravery?

3 What's the value of giving of ourselves along with the giving of the gospel?

4 Agree or disagree: The gospel is more than words. Why or why not?

WRAP-UP: DISCUSS HOW IT WOULD LOOK IN OUR WORKPLACES IF WE WERE TO GIVE OF OURSELVES AS WE GIVE THE GOSPEL.

 LET'S PRAY: (SEE PRAYER JOURNAL)

● ●

MY RESPONSE AS A PROMISE KEEPER

To what extent have I kept myself detached from my communication of the gospel at work? _____

_____

I will begin asking more questions of my fellow workers to show how much I care.

95

BARRIERS TO BOLDNESS

• •

WARM-UP:
AN UNSPOKEN RULE OF MANY BARBERSHOPS AND HAIR SALONS IS THAT TWO TOPICS ARE NEVER TO BE DISCUSSED THERE: RELIGION AND POLITICS. WHY IS THAT?

BACKGROUND

It's often difficult to discuss what matters most to us—our relationship with Jesus Christ. In today's session, we'll see that the followers of Christ in the first century also faced barriers in being ambassadors. How they handled them can help our witness in the workplace. As a group, take a few minutes to list the barriers you face on the job.

READ

ACTS 4:1-31

QUESTIONS FOR INTERACTION:

1 What were some of the barriers the early Christians faced as they sought to spread the Good News?

2 Why do you think the authorities erected barriers against the Christians?

3 What was so baffling to the authorities about the witness of the Christians?

4 What proved to be so effective among the early Christians in getting over the high barriers?

5 Agree or disagree: The early Christians should have obeyed the authorities, letting the quality of their lives be their only witness. Why or why not?

WRAP-UP: DISCUSS WHAT RESOURCES THE LORD PROVIDED FOR HIS FOLLOWERS THAT ARE STILL AVAILABLE FOR OUR EFFECTIVE WITNESS AND THE OVERCOMING OF BARRIERS.

 LET'S PRAY: (SEE PRAYER JOURNAL)

• •

MY RESPONSE AS A PROMISE KEEPER

For too long, I have focused on the barriers and not on the power of the Lord to make me an effective witness. Therefore, today I'm ready to cross some barriers by _____

_____

QUIZ SHOW

● ●

WARM-UP: FROM CHRISTIANITY'S EARLIEST DAYS, CRITICS AND SEEKERS ALIKE HAVE ASKED TOUGH QUESTIONS. "COULD GOD MAKE A ROCK SO BIG THAT HE COULDN'T MOVE IT?" "HOW COULD A LOVING GOD ALLOW EVIL AND SUFFERING?" "DON'T ALL RELIGIONS REALLY TEACH THE SAME THING?" "WHY DO CHRISTIANS SAY JESUS IS THE ONLY WAY TO GOD? THAT'S KIND OF NARROW, ISN'T IT?"

TOGETHER, LIST SOME OF THE TOUGH QUESTIONS YOU HEAR IN YOUR WORK WORLD CONCERNING THE CHRISTIAN FAITH.

BACKGROUND

Jesus demonstrated that questions are always welcome. But that means His followers must draw from His wisdom. Today we'll see the Lord in action, fielding hot questions and giving us pointers on how He did it.

READ

MARK 12:13-34

QUESTIONS FOR INTERACTION:

1 What are the possible motivators of questions fired at us? How can we sort out a person's motives?

2 When Jesus was questioned about paying taxes, what was so persuasive about His answer?

WALK
WORK
RELATIONSHIPS
MINISTRY

PK PROMISE KEEPERS®
MEN OF INTEGRITY

3 The Sadducees were skilled in asking tough questions. What was their question to Jesus? What do you like about the way He handled it?

4 Not all questions are meant to punch holes in what we believe. What was the wisdom of Jesus in answering the tough questions of the teacher of the law in verses 28-34? If you were that man, how would you feel after interacting with Jesus?

5 Jesus was knowledgeable about the issues, and also about the person or group asking the questions. How do you think He prepared Himself for such discussions?

WRAP-UP:
DISCUSS TOGETHER THREE OR FOUR PRINCIPLES JESUS APPARENTLY KEPT IN MIND AS HE FIELDED TOUGH QUESTIONS.

 LET'S PRAY: (SEE PRAYER JOURNAL)

MY RESPONSE AS A PROMISE KEEPER

"I, too, can field tough questions!" I can say this with growing confidence as I prepare myself by studying the issues and the audience around me.

I will increasingly welcome tough questions to help me communicate my faith better.

BATTERIES INCLUDED

• •

WARM-UP: ACCORDING TO SURVEYS, THE NUMBER-ONE FEAR OF ADULTS IS PUBLIC SPEAKING, FOLLOWED BY THE FEAR OF DYING. BUT AN EVEN GREATER FEAR THAN SPEAKING IN PUBLIC MAY WELL BE SPEAKING OUT ABOUT OUR FAITH IN JESUS CHRIST. DISCUSS TOGETHER WHAT CONTRIBUTES TO THOSE FEARS.

BACKGROUND

When it comes to telling our friends about Jesus, many of us feel uneasy and unsure of ourselves. As a result, we often say nothing. As long as we look to ourselves and our self-confidence, there will be a power problem. But there's a better way! In today's session, we can discover another source of power, beyond ourselves, that enables us to be winsome witnesses. The batteries are included!

READ

1 CORINTHIANS 2:1-12

QUESTIONS FOR INTERACTION:

1 If anyone could be confident in stating the basic facts of the gospel, it would be the apostle Paul. Why do you think he didn't draw on his self-confidence?

2 What problem did the apostle apparently have with using "lofty words or wisdom" in communicating the gospel? How might such expressions actually hinder our delivery of the message?

WALK
WORK
RELATIONSHIPS
MINISTRY

PK PROMISE
KEEPERS®
MEN OF INTEGRITY

3 If Paul was a picture of weakness and fear among the Corinthians, how was he able to communicate so effectively?

4 Who comes to mind among your friends as someone who witnesses in the Holy Spirit's power? What is that power like in this person?

WRAP-UP: THE GOAL IS TO SPEAK OUR WITNESS FOR CHRIST IN THE POWER OF THE HOLY SPIRIT, EVEN AS PAUL DID. TALK TOGETHER OF WAYS WE CAN DO THIS.

 LET'S PRAY: (SEE PRAYER JOURNAL)

. . . .

MY RESPONSE AS A PROMISE KEEPER

I am deciding today to no longer be a self-powered witness. From now on, I will pray to be filled with the Holy Spirit before I say anything for the Lord.

I am now looking for a Spirit-filled mentor to help me become an effective spokesman for the gospel.

PENETRATING THE PAGAN MIND

FOURTH IN THE SERIES ON EQUIPPED FOR WORKPLACE MINISTRY

• •

WARM-UP: IN COMMUNICATING THE GOSPEL IN OUR PLACES OF WORK, WE MAY THINK THERE ARE NO LONGER ANY MUTUAL POINTS OF INTEREST. BUT YOUR CO-WORKERS HAVE MORE IN COMMON WITH YOU THAN YOU MAY THINK. QUICKLY JOT DOWN 5 TO 10 THINGS YOU MAY HAVE IN COMMON WITH THEM. TALK TOGETHER ABOUT THE MANY ISSUES AND CONCERNS ALL WORKING PEOPLE SHARE.

BACKGROUND

The gospel rarely fails to make sense to those who hear it. But people fail to hear it because it hasn't been made relevant to their lives. The communicators of the Good News have failed their audience in not understanding their world. But in today's session, we have a classic story of someone so in touch with his audience that they actually invited him to speak!

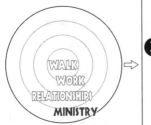

READ

ACTS 17:16-34

QUESTIONS FOR INTERACTION:

1 As the apostle Paul walked through Athens, what did he see? Why do you think that troubled him so deeply?

2 How did Paul relate to the various audiences surrounding him?

3 Why do you think Paul got the opportunity to speak publicly to the citizens of Athens? What made him so provocative?

4 If you were in the audience as Paul spoke, what would be of special interest or attractiveness to you? Why?

5 What were the three responses to Paul's presentation? (see verses 32-34) How can this be encouraging to us?

WRAP-UP: IF THE APOSTLE PAUL WERE TO WALK THROUGH YOUR WORKPLACE, WHAT IDOLS WOULD HE SEE? TALK TOGETHER OF WHAT YOU THINK HE WOULD TELL YOU TO DO ABOUT THEM.

LET'S PRAY: (SEE PRAYER JOURNAL)

● ●

MY RESPONSE AS A PROMISE KEEPER

I have failed to make the gospel relevant in my workplace. Today, I will attempt to see it as Paul saw Athens.

I am a Christian today in part because someone was able to demonstrate the relevance of Christ to me. I will seek to be that kind of person to _____ in my workplace.

AS IRON SHARPENS IRON

FIRST IN THE SERIES ON MULTIPLYING
A WORKPLACE MINISTRY

● ●

WARM-UP: THE MOST PROLIFIC SCORER IN THE HISTORY OF COLLEGE BASKETBALL WAS PISTOL PETE MARAVICH. WHEN ASKED, "PETE, HOW DID YOU LEARN TO SHOOT SO WELL?" HE RESPONDED, "MY DAD TAUGHT ME." TALK TOGETHER ABOUT A HOBBY, SPORT, OR VACATION IDEA THAT WAS TAUGHT TO YOU BY SOMEONE ELSE.

BACKGROUND

Have you wondered where the idea of spreading the Good News of new life in Jesus Christ originated? It's traceable back to the Scripture that's the focus of our session today. The last words of Jesus to His close followers were to "go and make disciples." What's a disciple? That question and others like it will lead us to discover the wonderful heritage we have to continue the spread of the gospel worldwide.

READ

MATTHEW 28:16-20

QUESTIONS FOR INTERACTION:

1 How did Jesus prepare the way for His followers to take His message to the world?

2 As we go, what are we to do? How would you define *disciple?*

3 What would be some indicators that we are fulfilling His challenge?

WALK
WORK
RELATIONSHIPS
MINISTRY

ACTS 9:10-19

1 What were the Lord's first steps in caring for this new Christian, Saul of Tarsus? What barriers did Ananias have to hurdle on his way to fulfilling the plan of Matthew 28?

2 What do you suppose would have happened to Saul if Ananias had refused to show the way to this new believer? Where do you think you would be today if someone had not discipled you? Where do you think you would be today if someone *had* tutored you initially?

"GIVEN THE TRADITIONAL WAY THAT MEN TEND TO PROCESS DEEPLY PERSONAL MATTERS, IT IS A FAIR GUESS THAT MOST MEN WILL TRY TO ANSWER THEIR QUESTIONS ALL BY THEMSELVES. HOWEVER, IF GIVEN A CHOICE, A VAST NUMBER WOULD GIVE ANYTHING FOR THE HELP OF AN OLDER MAN."

HOWARD HENDRICKS
AS IRON SHARPENS IRON

 WRAP-UP: DISCUSS TOGETHER WHAT MIGHT BE THE FIRST FEW STEPS TOWARD BEING INVOLVED IN ENCOURAGING NEW BELIEVERS.

LET'S PRAY: (SEE PRAYER JOURNAL)

MY RESPONSE AS A PROMISE KEEPER

I see the plan! Count me in! I make myself available to help fulfill the great challenge of Jesus to make disciples.

This is the first step I need to take toward being a discipler: _____

_____

ROOKIE CHRISTIAN

SECOND IN THE SERIES ON MULTIPLYING A WORKPLACE MINISTRY

● ●

WARM-UP:

LOU BECAME A CHRISTIAN AT A PROMISE KEEPERS CONFERENCE LAST SUMMER. AS HE TELLS HIS STORY, WE LEARN THAT PROFOUND CHANGES HAVE COME HIS WAY—NEW DESIRES, NEW HOPES, AND EVEN NEW FRIENDS. TALK TOGETHER ABOUT WHAT YOU FELT AND THOUGHT AS A NEW CHRISTIAN.

BACKGROUND

In our last session, we found Saul, a rookie Christian, in the care of available Ananias. The contrast in Saul's life was so great after he became a Christian that few, if any, believed the report of his conversion. What could he do? He desperately needed encouragement and teaching, but who would dare help this former vicious persecutor of Jesus' followers? Today's session highlights what can happen when we help new Christians get started in the faith.

WALK
WORK
RELATIONSHIPS
MINISTRY

READ

ACTS 9:20-31

QUESTIONS FOR INTERACTION:

1 Describe the person in your workplace you consider most unlikely to become a follower of Jesus Christ. (No names, please.) If he did become a believer, what could you do to encourage him?

2 Why do you think there was such reluctance, even fear, among the believers to welcome the report of Saul's new life?

3 Barnabas was a lifesaver for Saul. What do you think it took for him to step in and help Saul?

CONSIDER THIS:

THE NAME *BARNABAS* MEANS "SON OF ENCOURAGEMENT." HIS REAL NAME WAS JOE (JOSEPH; ACTS 4:36), BUT HE WAS SURNAMED BARNABAS BY THOSE WHO WATCHED HIM WORK WITH PEOPLE.

4 Barnabas was the second person to endorse Saul's new Christian experience. What were some of the benefits to Saul from those first two encouragers?

5 What might have happened to Saul if Barnabas had never shown up?

WRAP-UP: TALK TOGETHER OF EXAMPLES OF DISCIPLING YOU'VE SEEN IN THE MARKETPLACE. WHAT MADE THEM EFFECTIVE?

LET'S PRAY: (SEE PRAYER JOURNAL)

MY RESPONSE AS A PROMISE KEEPER

I will pray this month for the opportunity to meet new Christians, and I'll be an encouraging Barnabas to them.

If another new Christian is anything like me when I met the Lord, this person will especially need the following from me: _____

_____

"I Heard It Through the Grapevine"

THIRD IN THE SERIES ON MULTIPLYING A WORKPLACE MINISTRY

● ●

BACKGROUND

The greatest event in life is to become a Christian. But God doesn't stop there with us. His plan for our lives is one of growth toward maturity in all areas. What does it take for growth to occur? In part, it involves helping others grow as well. Today's session addresses these issues and more.

READ

JOHN 15:1-11

QUESTIONS FOR INTERACTION:

1 Vineyards were common to the region where Jesus lived, so He used a vine and its branches to illustrate how His followers can grow. With a vineyard in mind, what produces growth in our lives as His followers?

2 The significance of the vineyard is not branches alone, but fruit on them. In the same way, Jesus said fruit-bearing is everything. Why?

3 If your disciple were to ask you, "What does 'remaining in Christ' mean?" how would you answer?

CONSIDER THIS:

"LEFT TO ITSELF, A VINE WILL PRODUCE A GOOD DEAL OF UNPRODUCTIVE GROWTH. FOR MAXIMUM FRUITFULNESS, EXTENSIVE PRUNING IS ESSENTIAL."

A VINEYARD KEEPER

4 If there's little or no growth in one of our disciples, what might be the hindrance? How can we help growth to be restored?

5 According to Jesus, what does it take to be a joyful person?

WRAP-UP: TOGETHER DESCRIBE CHARACTERISTICS (NOT ACTIVITIES) OF ONE OF OUR DISCIPLES WHO IS GROWING IN CHRIST.

LET'S PRAY: (SEE PRAYER JOURNAL)

MY RESPONSE AS A PROMISE KEEPER

I will reread this passage today, focusing on my own remaining (or abiding) in Christ.

I will reread this passage again today, focusing on _____ (name of new Christian) as I encourage him to remain in Christ.

GOD'S FAMILY

FOURTH IN THE SERIES ON MULTIPLYING A WORKPLACE MINISTRY

• •

WARM-UP: IT'S BEEN ALMOST A YEAR SINCE AL BECAME A CHRISTIAN AT A PROMISE KEEPERS EVENT. THERE HE WAS ENCOURAGED TO GET INVOLVED IN THE CHURCH. HE AND HIS FAMILY ARE SO THANKFUL TO BE A PART OF A LOCAL CONGREGATION. DISCUSS TOGETHER WHAT YOUR CHURCHES OFFER TO WELCOME AND NURTURE MEN LIKE AL.

BACKGROUND

It should be no surprise that our final Promise Builders session lands us right where Jesus left us— in the hands of each other, the church. The church is God's family. And like the other families of which we're a part, it not only contributes to our lives, but it rightfully has expectations of us as well. Today's session can be a time of fresh insight into how God's church is meant to be a center for encouraging us in our growth.

READ

EPHESIANS 3:7-21

QUESTIONS FOR INTERACTION:

1 What are biological families intended to contribute to their members? What should a family expect from its members?

2 The church is made up of brothers and sisters in Christ. To keep this family strong, what does it need from me? What can it provide for me?

3 The apostle Paul was a leader in the church of the first century. What are leaders like him directed to do for the church?

4 What place do you think the Lord desires the church to have in the lives of new Christians?

5 Many people are critical of the church. Why is it especially vulnerable to criticism? What are some good ways to communicate our support of our churches?

WRAP-UP: WHY DO YOU GO TO CHURCH? WHAT DOES IT DO BEST FOR NEW CHRISTIANS? WHAT COULD IT DO BETTER?

 LET'S PRAY: (SEE PRAYER JOURNAL)

MY RESPONSE AS A PROMISE KEEPER

I may have underestimated the church's place in my life. This week I am going to start taking my commitment to it more seriously, and my first change is to _____

My pastor may not know I'm on his team. I will communicate my support by _____

PROMISE BUILDERS

PRAYER JOURNAL

DATE	PRAYER REQUEST	FROM	ANSWER

PROMISE BUILDERS

PRAYER JOURNAL

DATE	PRAYER REQUEST	FROM	ANSWER

PROMISE BUILDERS

P R A Y E R   J O U R N A L

DATE	PRAYER REQUEST	FROM	ANSWER

PROMISE BUILDERS

PRAYER JOURNAL

DATE	PRAYER REQUEST	FROM	ANSWER

PROMISE BUILDERS

P R A Y E R   J O U R N A L

DATE	PRAYER REQUEST	FROM	ANSWER

PROMISE BUILDERS

PRAYER JOURNAL

DATE	PRAYER REQUEST	FROM	ANSWER

PROMISE BUILDERS

PRAYER JOURNAL

DATE	PRAYER REQUEST	FROM	ANSWER

PROMISE BUILDERS

PRAYER JOURNAL

DATE	PRAYER REQUEST	FROM	ANSWER

PROMISE BUILDERS

PRAYER JOURNAL

DATE	PRAYER REQUEST	FROM	ANSWER

ADDITIONAL RESOURCES

AVAILABLE FROM PROMISE KEEPERS

PERIODICALS & STUDY TOOLS

GO THE DISTANCE
(Colorado Springs, Colo.: Focus on the Family, 1996)

THE POWER OF A PROMISE KEPT
Gregg Lewis (Colorado Springs, Colo.: Focus on the Family, 1995)

SEVEN PROMISES OF A PROMISE KEEPER
(Colorado Springs, Colo.: Focus on the Family, 1994)
Also available on four 90-minute audiocassettes.

STRATEGIES FOR A SUCCESSFUL MARRIAGE: A STUDY GUIDE FOR MEN
E. Glenn Wagner, Ph. D. (Colorado Springs, Colo.: NavPress, 1994)

FOCUSING YOUR MEN'S MINISTRY
Peter A. Richardson (Denver: Promise Keepers, 1993)

BROTHERS! CALLING MEN INTO VITAL RELATIONSHIPS
Geoff Gorsuch and Dan Schaffer (Denver: Promise Keepers, 1993)

DAILY DISCIPLINES FOR THE CHRISTIAN MAN
Bob Beltz (Colorado Springs, Colo.: NavPress, 1993)

WHAT GOD DOES WHEN MEN PRAY
William Carr Peel (Colorado Springs, Colo.: NavPress, 1993)

WHAT IS A PROMISE KEEPER?
(Denver: Promise Keepers, 1993)
Available in audiocassette only.

WHAT MAKES A MAN? & STUDY GUIDE
Bill McCartney (Colorado Springs, Colo.: NavPress, 1992)

BREAK DOWN THE WALLS
Maranatha! Promise Band (Laguna Hills, Calif.: 1996)
Available in: Compact Disc
                  Audiocassette

FAVORITE HYMNS OF PROMISE KEEPERS AND THE MARANATHA! PROMISE BAND
(Laguna Hills, Calif.: 1996)
Available in: Compact Disc
                  Audiocassette

LIVE WORSHIP WITH PROMISE KEEPERS AND THE MARANATHA! PROMISE BAND
(Laguna Hills, Calif.: 1996)
Available in: Compact Disc
                  Audiocassette

RAISE THE STANDARD
Maranatha! Music (Laguna Hills, Calif.: 1995)
Available in: Compact Disc
                  Audiocassette

PK LIVE: WORSHIP TAPE
Maranatha! Music (Laguna Hills, Calif.: 1994)
Available in: Compact Disc
                  Audiocassette

SEIZE THE MOMENT: WORSHIP FOR MEN
Maranatha! Music (Laguna Hills, Calif.: 1994)
Available in: Compact Disc
                  Audiocassette

PROMISE KEEPERS: A LIFE THAT SHOWS
Sparrow (Brentwood, Tenn.: 1994)
Available in: Compact Disc
                  Audiocassette
                  Songbook

FACE TO FACE: WORSHIP FOR MEN

Maranatha! Music (Laguna Hills, Calif.: 1993)

Available in: Compact Disc

                      Audiocassette

                      Songbook

                      Words Only

FOR ADDITIONAL INFORMATION AND RESOURCES

Call: 1-800-456-7594

Or write to: Promise Keepers

                  P. O. Box 18376

                  Boulder, CO 80308

Jude Doxology

And now all glory to Him who alone is God
who saves us through His Son, Jesus Christ, the Lord
For He is able to keep us from falling away
He brings us into His presence with love and joy

All power, authority, all splendor and majesty
Are His from the beginning and evermore, and evermore
All power, authority, all splendor and majesty
Are His from the beginning and evermore, and evermore

And now all glory to you, you alone are God
You've saved us through your Son, Jesus Christ, the Lord
For you are able to keep us from falling away.
You bring us into your presence with love and joy

All power, authority, all splendor and majesty
Are yours from the beginning and evermore, and evermore
All power, authority, all splendor and majesty
Are yours from the beginning and evermore, and evermore

c. 1991   Mercy/Vineyard Publications

Jude Doxology

And now all glory to Him who alone is God
Who save us through His Son, Jesus Christ, the Lord
For He is able to keep us from falling away
He brings us into his presence with love and joy

All power, authority, all splendor and majesty
Are His from the beginning and evermore..and evermore
All power, authority, all splendor and majesty
Are His from the beginning and evermore...and evermore

And now all glory to you, you alone are God
You've saved us through your Son, Jesus Christ, our Lord
For you are able to keep us from falling away
You bring us into your presence with love and joy

All power, authority, all splendor and majesty
Are yours from the beginning and evermore... and evermore
All power, authority, all splendor and majesty
Are yours from the beginning and evermore... and evermore

c. 1991   Mercy/Vineyard Publications

I GIVE THANKS

You have shown me favor unending
You have given your life for me
And my heart   knows of your goodness
Your blood has covered me

> I will arise and give thanks to you Lord, my God
> And your name I will bless with my whole heart
> You have shown mercy, You have shown mercy to me
> I give thanks to you, Lord

You have poured out your healing upon us
You have set the captives free
And we know it's not what we've done
But by your hand alone

> I will arise and give thanks to you Lord, my God
> And your name I will bless with my whole heart
> You have shown mercy, You have shown mercy to me
> I give thanks to you, Lord

> > You, oh Lord, are the healer of our soul
> > You, oh Lord are the Gracious Redeemer
> > You come to restore us again
> > Yes, you come to restore us again.... and again

You have shown me favor unending
You have given your life for me
And my heart   knows of your goodness
Your blood has covered me

> I will arise and give thanks to you Lord, my God
> And your name I will bless with my whole heart
> You have shown mercy, You have shown mercy to me
> I give thanks to you, Lord

c. 1991 Mercy/Vineyard Publications